Welcome to America?
A Pro/Con Debate Over Immigration

Tom Streissguth

Enslow Publishers, Inc.
40 Industrial Road
Box 398
Berkeley Heights, NJ 07922
USA

http://www.enslow.com

Library of Congress Cataloging-in-Publication Data

Streissguth, Thomas, 1958–
    Welcome to America? : a pro/con debate over immigration / Tom Streissguth.
      p. cm. — (Issues in focus today)
    Summary: "Examines immigration in the United States, including the history of U.S. immigration and the debate over immigration reforms, laws, and policies"—Provided by publisher.
    Includes bibliographical references and index.
    ISBN-13: 978-0-7660-2912-5
    ISBN-10: 0-7660-2912-3
    1. United States—Emigration and immigration—Juvenile literature. 2. United States—Emigration and immigration—History—Juvenile literature. 3. United States—Emigration and immigration—Government policy—Juvenile literature. 4. United States—Emigration and immigration—Economic aspects—Juvenile literature. 5. Emigration and immigration law—United States—Juvenile literature. 6. Illegal aliens—United States—Juvenile literature. 7. Americanization—Juvenile literature. 8. Assimilation (Sociology)—United States—Juvenile literature. 9. Border security—United States—Juvenile literature. I. Title.
    JV6465.S84 2009
    325.73—dc22   2007046080

Printed in the United States of America

10 9 8 7 6 5 4 3 2 1

To Our Readers: We have done our best to make sure all Internet Addresses in this book were active and appropriate when we went to press. However, the author and the publisher have no control over and assume no liability for the material available on those Internet sites or on other Web sites they may link to. Any comments or suggestions can be sent by e-mail to comments@enslow.com or to the address on the back cover.

♲ Enslow Publishers, Inc., is committed to printing our books on recycled paper. The paper in every book contains 10% to 30% post-consumer waste (PCW). The cover board on the outside of each book contains 100% PCW. Our goal is to do our part to help young people and the environment too!

Illustration Credits: Ansel Adams/Library of Congress, p. 25; AP/Wide World, pp. 50, 66; courtesy of Steven Chichon, pp. 3, 9; courtesy of Carolina Galindo, p. 60; Library of Congress, pp. 3, 5, 15, 19, 21, 86, 105; courtesy of Jenna Norwood, p. 17; Michael Riger/FEMA News Photo, p. 71; courtesy of Rachel Robinson, pp. 23; courtesy of Sarasota Historical Society, p. 12; Shutterstock, pp. 1, 3, 31, 39, 43, 46, 53, 57, 80, 89, 96, 101; U.S. Customs and Border Protection, pp. 3, 34, 68, 75, 78, 84, 93, 103.

Cover Illustration: Library of Congress (large photo); BananaStock (inset photo)

C o n t e n t s

A Land of Newcomers

It was the first day of the year 1892. A fifteen-year-old girl waited at the gangplank of the ship, ahead of two brothers. The three of them were at the front of a long line of hopeful, tired people. They had come a long way from their homes across the sea in Ireland. Now Annie stood at the front gate of America, Ellis Island.

A small crowd of officials was there to greet her. To honor her achievement, they offered her a ten-dollar gold coin. Annie Moore was the first immigrant to pass through Ellis Island in New York harbor. She would live in New York, get married, and give birth to eleven children. Hopeful people from all over Europe followed her to Ellis Island. In all, more than

100 million people living in the United States have ancestors who passed through Ellis Island to settle in America.

The First Immigrants

The first immigrants to North America walked to their new country. About 30,000 years ago, nomadic hunters crossed a bridge of land that once connected Alaska and Siberia. Over many millennia, they spread throughout the western hemisphere. They divided into nations and smaller groups. These people, the American Indians, adapted to their new environments. Some settled and became farmers. Others kept on the move in search of food.

North America was unknown to Europeans until the tenth century A.D., when Viking sailors arrived on the northern coast of Newfoundland. The Vikings came from Iceland and Norway. They built a small settlement at L'Anse aux Meadows (a name related to "Jellyfish Cove" in French). Although the land and climate were good, the Vikings fought with the Indians. After a short time, they abandoned the settlement.

In the late fifteenth century, Europeans returned to North America. Christopher Columbus, an Italian ship captain, led a fleet of three small ships to the Bahamas in 1492. Columbus was searching for a route to the East Indies, islands in southeast Asia that were a source of valuable spices. Instead, the Europeans realized Columbus had discovered an entirely new continent. The kings and queens of Europe sent more fleets to explore North America.

In the sixteenth century, the first English settlers came to North Carolina and Virginia. In the 1600s, English Puritans settled in Massachusetts, seeking the freedom to practice their faith. They were followed by French, German, and Dutch settlers, who found new homes along the Atlantic seaboard of North America.

Massachusetts and the other English colonies needed laborers.

Workshops in Boston and New York did not have enough employees. In Virginia and Maryland, tobacco farms needed people to plant and harvest the crop. The indenture system and the practice of "redemption" filled part of this need.

In return for their passage across the Atlantic Ocean, indentured servants allowed ship captains to sell their labor to buyers in the New World. The contract bound an indentured servant to several years of work. The indenture system survived until early in the nineteenth century. It provided an opportunity for the poor people of England and Europe to begin anew in the colonies.

"Redemptioners" agreed to work in order to pay back a loan for their passage. One German redemptioner, Gottlieb Mittleberger, described the scene as redemptioners arrived in a New World port in 1750:

> Every day Englishmen, Dutchmen and High-German people come from the city of Philadelphia and other places . . . adult persons bind themselves in writing to serve three, four, five, or six years for the amount due by them, according to their age and strength. But very young people, from 10 to 15 years, must serve till they are 21 years old.[1]

African slaves also provided labor in the colonies. Ships carried captive slaves in chains from West Africa to North America. Slave markets at American harbors allowed buyers to examine and bid for men, women, and children. The cross-Atlantic slave trade continued until the U.S. government banned it in 1808. Slavery itself did not end until the Civil War.

To those who did not need the indenture system, joint-stock companies advertised the virtues of the new land. The English government gave these companies the right to populate the colonies. The companies needed able-bodied men and women to settle territory in North America. They needed farmers to work the land and artisans to produce goods in the cities. The companies brought immigrants to North America, and then shipped food, cotton, indigo, tobacco, and merchandise from the colonies to the home country for sale.

The First Immigration Laws

There were few limits on immigration in colonial America. The colonies needed laborers and artisans from Europe: blacksmiths, for example, as well as wheelwrights, bakers, silversmiths, and printers. But most of the colonies banned former criminals. Port cities also imposed quarantines on arriving ships. The quarantines confined people with contagious diseases. After independence, many states passed laws barring people "likely to become a public charge." This included people who could not work at all. They might have been blind or disabled in some other way. They may have had a disease, such as tuberculosis. Those who could not work had to depend on charity to survive. Towns and counties paid for public poorhouses, orphanages, and asylums. The costs were borne by local taxpayers.

In 1798, the United States Congress passed the Alien Friends Act. This law gave the president the authority during peacetime to arrest and deport without evidence anyone considered dangerous. Another law, the Alien Enemies Act, allowed the president to deport aliens from enemy countries during wartime.

Many lawmakers strongly opposed the acts. They did not feel that Congress had the authority to restrict immigration. Instead, immigration law was the business of the states. In 1800, the Alien Friends Act was allowed to lapse. The Alien Enemies Act is still in force, more than two hundred years after becoming law.

Living in America

Most immigrants were young. Many were unmarried and without families. It was common for single men from the working classes of Europe to leave home and take their chances in North

America. They had no land and little opportunity at home. Many of these bachelors married in the United States, then invited other family members to immigrate. This "chain migration" brought large families, and sometimes entire villages, across the Atlantic.

Certain neighborhoods of the United States became tight-knit immigrant communities. A group of German families from the town of Krefeld built the city of Germantown, Pennsylvania. Immigrants from Germany followed the Krefelders into the Pennsylvania colony over the next century. Confusingly, they became known as "Pennsylvania Dutch," from the German word *Deutsch*, which means "German."

In many neighborhoods, people still used the language of their home country. They had their own stores. They read newspapers in their native language, and they formed clubs. The Charitable Irish Society formed in 1737, the Hibernian Society

Jaku Jancura, who came from Poland, stands among his stock on his Ohio chicken farm. Tight-knit immigrant communities formed all over the United States.

(for Irish Americans) in 1790, and the Sons of Hermann (for German Americans) in New York City in the 1840s. These clubs allowed immigrants to help each other and to keep traditions from the Old World alive.

Maintaining ethnic identity was a point of pride for many immigrants. At the same time, some who were born in the United States saw this ethnic pride as a threat to American traditions. They wanted immigrants to assimilate to the customs of the United States and to leave their language and traditions behind.

The Irish Arrive

In the first years of the nineteenth century, population was increasing rapidly in Ireland. By the 1840s, Ireland's population was eight million. Irish farmers worked tiny plots of land. Many relied on potatoes, a plant imported from the Americas. Potatoes were hardy plants and provided basic nutrition. Many Irish families ate potatoes and little else.

Young Irishmen began leaving their poverty-stricken homeland for Canada. They worked in lumber camps and in port cities. But better opportunities in the northeastern United States convinced many Irish-Canadians to journey south to New England. They took riverboats, if they could afford the fare. Otherwise, they walked.

Immigration by the Irish-Canadians created the first Irish communities in Boston and other New England cities. Irishmen worked hard and sent money home. If they saved enough, they helped other family members pay for the Atlantic passage.

Irish workers found jobs in the burgeoning industries of the northeast. They were hired as policemen, firemen, and civil servants. They banded together to establish powerful political groups.

Many Irish women worked as domestic servants. Very few

native-born Americans would work as servants. This created a high demand for British and Irish maids, who could speak English. Irish women also worked in the textile industry and as laundresses and seamstresses.

Then, in 1846, disaster struck in Ireland. A blight (disease) destroyed the Irish potato crop. With the entire harvest ruined, Irish farmers had to eat their seed potatoes in order to survive. In the following years, they had no seeds to plant. In a short time, more than a million Irish died of starvation and disease.

> **Maintaining ethnic identity was a point of pride for many immigrants, but some who were born in the United States saw this as a threat to American traditions.**

The potato blight began a great wave of Irish immigration to the United States. About two million Irish men, women, and children fled to America in the 1840s and 1850s. These immigrants braved hazardous conditions at sea, where disease raged through the filthy, unsafe vessels.

The dangers did not discourage the Irish. One immigrant, Margaret McCarthy, wrote home in 1850: "Any man or woman are fools that would not venture and come to this plentyful Country where no man or woman ever hungered or ever will and where you will not be seen naked."[2]

The Nativist Movement

The territory of the United States steadily expanded westward. In 1848, the Treaty of Guadalupe Hidalgo ended the Mexican-American War. By this treaty, the United States took possession of territory that would become California, Nevada, and Utah, and parts of Arizona, New Mexico, Colorado, and Wyoming. In the meantime, a great wave of immigrants began arriving. In 1842, 100,000 came; five years later immigrants numbered 200,000. In 1854 there were 400,000. In the 1840s and 1850s, the Irish made up nearly half of all immigrants.[3]

Not everyone welcomed the Irish. Some newspaper advertisements seeking workers said, "No Irish Need Apply." The fact that many Irish (and some German) immigrants were Roman Catholic angered some native-born Americans. They saw the Protestant heritage of the country slipping away. Protestants, in this view, would soon become a minority in their own country.

Public opinion on immigration started to change. The wave of Irish Catholics who arrived in the 1840s inspired an anti-immigrant movement. The members of this "nativist" movement were strongly opposed to Irish immigration. They saw the Irish as shiftless, lazy, and more prone to crime and alcoholism. Nativists organized into what became the American Party and fielded candidates for political office. They controlled who could join the group and kept their organization secret. When asked about the group, members told outsiders "I know nothing!"

A group of Scottish immigrants photographed in Florida in 1916. Public opinion on immigration started to change in the late nineteenth century with the growth of the Nativist movement.

The American—or "Know-Nothing"—Party believed Catholic immigrants did not belong in the United States. In this view, Catholics owed their loyalty to their church first and their country second, and they would undermine American traditions on the orders of the pope, the head of the Catholic Church. The Irish, according to this view, owed allegiance to the pope, not the American government.

The Know Nothings demanded higher bars to citizenship. They also believed foreign-born people should not be allowed to hold political office. Their party grew strong in cities with large immigrant populations. Riots targeted Catholic institutions, monasteries, and churches.

Nativists also made an issue of language. They demanded that English be the country's official language. In early America, many public schools taught in German as well as English. Cincinnati had two school systems, one using German and the other English. German instruction was supposed to bring more children into the public school system. But many people opposed it, because they believed all Americans should learn English, the dominant language.

The Fourteenth Amendment, ratified in 1868, declared that all those born in the United States became American citizens. Former slaves, as well as children born to immigrants on U.S. soil, now had the name and the rights of citizens. But new federal laws were also restricting immigration and naturalization (citizenship) of the foreign-born. Asian immigrants, no matter how long they lived in the United States, could not become citizens.

Immigration laws, once the business of the states, became the subject of federal laws, which were in effect throughout the country. In 1875, the U.S. Congress barred the door to foreign convicts and prostitutes. Later statutes excluded the mentally ill, those with contagious diseases, polygamists, and anyone convicted of a crime of moral turpitude. An immigrant could be labeled "likely to become a public charge" and sent back to the home country.

A New Wave

In the meantime, a new wave of immigration was taking place on the west coast of the United States. Chinese laborers were recruited to work as miners and in construction gangs, and to help build the railroads that linked the western regions with the rest of the country. In smaller numbers, Japanese and Filipinos were also immigrating to the West Coast. The Chinese and other Asian immigrants set up ethnic enclaves in San Francisco and other cities. They did not mix with the non-Asian population.

New federal laws were restricting immigration and naturalization of the foreign-born. Asian immigrants, no matter how long they lived in the United States, could not become citizens.

The Chinese, in particular, kept to themselves. They lived in tight-knit communities where outsiders were not welcome. To native-born Americans, they spoke a strange language, dressed differently, and followed a completely foreign religion. They also competed for jobs.

In the case of *Chae Chan Ping* v. *United States*, the U.S. Supreme Court upheld restrictions on Chinese immigration. In his written opinion, one justice stated:

> [The Chinese] remained strangers in the land, residing apart by themselves, and adhering to the customs and usages of their own country. It seemed impossible for them to assimilate with our people or to make any change in their habits or modes of living. As they grew in numbers each year the people of the [west] coast saw . . . great danger that at no distant day that portion of our country would be overrun by them unless prompt action was taken to restrict their immigration.[4]

Senator James G. Blaine repeated this opinion in a speech he made on the floor of the U.S. Senate:

Many people from China, Japan, and the Philippines emigrated to the United States in the early 1900s. These children were photographed celebrating Chinese New Year in New York City in 1909.

Either the Anglo-Saxon race will possess the Pacific slope or the Mongolians will possess it. . . . We have this day to choose . . . whether our legislation shall be in the interest of the American free laborer or for the servile laborer from China. . . . You cannot work a man who must have beef and bread, and would prefer beer, alongside of a man who can live on rice. It cannot be done.[5]

Anti-Chinese opinion resulted in the Chinese Exclusion Act of 1882, which suspended immigration of all Chinese except merchants for ten years. If they wanted to leave temporarily, the Chinese could get a certificate that allowed them back into the United States. In 1888, however, Congress cancelled these certificates, stranding thousands of legal immigrants in China. The Chinese Exclusion Act was renewed in 1892 and made permanent in 1902. (It would finally be overturned in 1943, when China was allied with the United States during World War II.) Despite the law, many Chinese came to the United States. They were the first to come illegally in large numbers from a single country. Most came as stowaways aboard ships. They braved a long ocean crossing to get to California. Mines, railroads, and farms in the west needed their labor. Employers did not ask for official papers, passports, or work permits. The employers set up camps where Chinese workers lived, apart from the others.

The Ellis Island Experience

Southern and eastern Europe supplied most of the new immigrants on the east coast. In the late nineteenth century, the so-called Lower East Side of New York City attracted European Jews. The Jews came mostly from eastern Europe and Russia. Many of them worked in retail and banking industries. Some were peddlers or pawnshop owners—professions familiar to them from the Old World.

At the same time, Italians were fleeing poverty in their homeland and taking up residence in America's urban centers. Poles, Czechs, Slovaks, Greeks, Armenians, Hungarians, and

Russians flooded into eastern port cities. Local officials in New York could not handle the growing crowds of foreigners. In 1892, a federal immigration center opened on Ellis Island in New York harbor. Ellis Island operated for sixty-two years and processed some 12 million immigrants.[6]

Passing through Ellis Island could be a terrifying experience. The United States had laws barring certain people from entering the country—laws immigrants knew little about when they left home. Doctors at Ellis Island gave everyone a careful examination. Anyone found to have a contagious disease could be stopped, kept in a dormitory, and then sent home. The Ellis Island arrivals also had to have a sponsor. If they did not have a relative in the United States to vouch for them, they could not enter the country.

People stuck on Ellis Island could do nothing but wander the halls of the immigration center. One eyewitness reported:

> I saw people that had not arrived with us or come later or anything, people who seemed to have been living there, for I don't know how long. You know, they were used to all this. They were wandering around. They didn't have suitcases. They appeared to have room and board, because they couldn't get out for one reason or another. The inspection was really very strict in those days.[7]

Gennaro DeLuca was one of millions to enter the United States through Ellis Island. A concert pianist, he came to America from Naples, Italy, in 1913. He was an aerial photographer for the U.S. Army during World War I.

Labor vs. Business

In the late nineteenth century, many new factories were operating in the eastern United States. Immigrants made up a large percentage of low-wage factory workers. Women worked in the clothing industry. The steel industry employed many eastern and southern European immigrants. Many of these jobs were unskilled. The jobs did not require any experience or training.

Skilled laborers commanded higher wages. They also formed unions to protect their interests. As immigration increased, labor unions began to protest. They saw competition for jobs holding down wages. More people demanding work meant that employers could pay workers less. Employers could also resist union demands for shorter hours and better working conditions.

Passing through Ellis Island could be a terrifying experience. U.S. laws barred certain people from entering the country—laws immigrants knew little about when they left home.

Business owners wanted to keep wages low. The less they paid their workers, the higher the profit on the goods they made. They were competing against each other and against foreign companies. Employers wanted a ready supply of unskilled, low-wage workers. They were generally against limits on immigration.

An economic debate on immigration began. This debate did not involve the nationality of new immigrants. It involved the competing interests of workers and business owners. Most skilled workers sought limits on immigration, while business owners wanted cheap labor and open borders. The two sides continue to debate the issue in the same way, and with similar opinions, in the twenty-first century.

A Mexican family entering the United States in 1938.

Twentieth-Century Immigration

In the 1890s, the United States experienced an economic depression. Unemployment became a serious problem in the cities. Some blamed unskilled immigrants, who competed for low-paying jobs in manufacturing industries. Labor unions raised the call for more restrictions on immigration.

At this time, new kinds of immigrants were arriving at Ellis Island. Most of the newcomers were from southern or eastern Europe. They were Italians, Poles, Greeks, Jews, and Slavs. There were more people from southern Europe than from Britain, Germany, and Scandinavia.

The Immigration Restriction League formed in 1894 to

oppose the immigration of what they considered undesirable groups. This organization influenced many members of Congress. Seeking to limit the number of new immigrants, in 1897 Congress passed a literacy test. However, President Grover Cleveland vetoed the test.

Many people also worried about the effect of dangerous radicals arriving from abroad. Socialists and anarchists (who opposed all forms of government) were stirring up revolt in Europe. Legislators in Congress saw this as a threat to the United States. A new law was prompted by the assassination of President William McKinley in 1901 by Leon Czolgosz, an anarchist and the son of Polish immigrants. In 1903, Congress officially barred anarchists from immigrating to the United States.

On the west coast, native-born Americans saw Asian immigrants as a threat to their culture and their livelihoods. In California, Japanese immigrants were hired to work picking fruits and vegetables, and in factories and construction. But the influx of Japanese also caused friction in large cities such as San Francisco, where all Asian students were forced to attend segregated (separate) schools. By the Gentlemen's Agreement of 1907, Japan agreed to stop the flow of immigrants to the United States. In return, President Theodore Roosevelt persuaded the city of San Francisco to end its discrimination against Japanese schoolchildren.

The tide of immigration turned into a flood in the early years of the twentieth century. Then, in 1914, World War I began in Europe. Germany invaded France. The war drew in Great Britain, Italy, Austria-Hungary, and Russia. Immigration from Europe came to a halt.

Many people in the United States saw Germany as the aggressor in the war. The United States government, which supported the cause of France and Britain against Germany, stayed out of the war at first. German-Americans, in particular, did not want their adopted country to get involved.

In 1917, a secret telegram came to light. Arthur Zimmerman, the German foreign minister, had sent the message to the government of Mexico. Zimmerman invited Mexico to "make war together, make peace together . . . and [with] an understanding on our part that Mexico is to reconquer the lost territory in Texas, New Mexico and Arizona."[1]

Germany had been arming the Mexican rebel Pancho Villa. With a small band of guerrillas, Villa was crossing the southern border of the United States and attacking towns and ranches in New Mexico.

The Zimmerman telegram and the raids of Pancho Villa inspired anger and fear throughout the United States. Many

Sacco and Vanzetti were two Italian immigrants—and avowed anarchists— accused of a robbery and murder in Massachusetts. Although the evidence against them was weak, they were convicted and executed. Americans' concerns about anarchists and prejudice against Italians are believed to have contributed to the unfairness of their trial.

people suspected that Mexico, with Germany's help, was trying to reconquer the southwestern United States.

The United States entered the war against Germany in 1917. American troops sailed to Europe to fight in northern France. German submarines prowled the North Atlantic, attacking freighters and passenger ships.

The federal government issued new rules on the rights of German-born males over the age of 14. They could not own arms or ammunition, and they could not live near a military installation. They were considered "enemy aliens" and had to register with the government. Washington, D.C., was off-limits to all German-born men and women.

New Immigration Law

The end of World War I did not end hostility to immigrants. A revolution in Russia inspired great fear of political radicals. The U.S. government arrested thousands of foreign-born residents. Attorney General A. Mitchell Palmer directed these "Palmer Raids," which targeted socialists and communists. Thousands of people were held without being charged with any crime.

There were calls for new restrictions on immigration. Congress studied a plan to place quotas on people from certain nations. The plan had been created by the United States Immigration Commission of 1909–1911, also known as the Dillingham Commission.

The plan restricted the total number of immigrants. But not all nationalities were treated equally. The plan freely allowed immigration from the Western Hemisphere (Canada and Latin America). But immigrants from Europe would be limited to 5 percent of the foreign-born U.S. residents from those countries, according to the census of 1910. If the census had reported the presence of 100,000 French-Americans, for example, then only 5,000 French people would be granted permission to immigrate each year.

The Dillingham Commission plan was an attempt to keep the ethnic mix of the United States as it had been in 1910. It favored a northern European melting pot, and tried to keep out people from southern and eastern Europe.

While accepting the Dillingham Comission plan, the House of Representatives lowered the census quotas to 3 percent. An immigration bill passed but was vetoed by President Woodrow Wilson. His successor, President Warren Harding, signed the Emergency Quota Act, also known as the Johnson Act, in 1921. The total number of immigrants to be admitted each year was 357,803. There were to be 200,000 northern Europeans admitted, and 155,000 newcomers from southern and eastern Europe.[2]

John and Albert Newell came to West Virginia from the British Isles and worked as coal miners during the 1920s. Beginning in the early part of the twentieth century, quotas limited the number of people who could immigrate from different countries.

The National Origins Quota Act of 1924 changed the census quotas again. By this law, the quotas for Europeans were reduced to 2 percent. The 1890 census would be used for determining the quota numbers. By 1927, the permanent annual quota of immigrants allowed from all of Europe would be 165,000. In addition, by the new concept of "national origins," the law counted the portion of the population with a specific national origin that had settled in the United States since the year 1790. This was an attempt to keep an Anglo-American majority in the United States.[3] The laws ended the high tide of immigration that had begun in the 1890s.

In 1929, as the new laws were taking effect, the stock market crashed. The American economy nearly ground to a stop. Trade fell drastically. Unemployment ran high, and many businesses closed their doors. Millions of families lost their savings and their homes. The quota law, meanwhile, resulted in much less immigration from Europe, especially from southern and eastern Europe. Some foreign-born people returned to their homelands.

Enemy Aliens

War clouds were gathering again in Europe. Germany raised new armies and threatened its former enemies. In 1939, the United States created the Custodial Detention Index. This was a list of Germans, Italians, and communists who were subject to arrest in case of war. In September, Germany attacked Poland and World War II began in Europe.

In June 1940, Congress passed the Smith Act. All aliens over the age of fourteen had to register with the Immigration and Naturalization Service (INS). By law, they also had to provide a statement of their beliefs. They had to report any change of address and register again every three months.

In December 1941, the Japanese navy attacked Pearl Harbor, Hawaii. This was an important American naval base in the middle of the Pacific Ocean. In response to this attack on a U.S. territory (Hawaii was not yet a state), the United States declared war on Japan, Germany, and Italy. U.S. forces were deployed to the Pacific, Europe, and North Africa during World War II.

All aliens had to carry ID cards, move away from coastal areas, and obey curfews. President Franklin Roosevelt signed Executive Order 9066, authorizing internment camps (temporary prison camps). West Coast Exclusion Zones were set up, banning people of Japanese ancestry from living anywhere in California. More than 100,000 Japanese were interned for the duration of the war. Most of them were U.S. citizens. Nevertheless, they were suspected of undermining the war effort. Historian Michele Wucker, in her history of immigration, *Lockout*, reports:

Thousands of Japanese Americans were forced into internment camps during World War II. Here, people at Manzanar War Relocation Center in California walk to their barracks after church.

Wild accusations were made—for example, that Japanese gardeners were hiding short-wave transmitters in their garden hoses; that Japanese were poisoning vegetables sold in the market and contaminating cans of Japanese seafood with ground glass.[4]

Although Germany and Italy were official enemies of the United States as well, German-Americans and Italian-Americans were allowed their freedom during the war. In addition, the Chinese were rewarded for their country's alliance with the United States against Japan. In 1943, Congress repealed the Chinese Exclusion Act. A small number of Chinese were allowed to immigrate. In 1946, the law also established small quotas for people from the Philippines, which had won independence from the United States, and from India. In the eyes of the U.S. Congress, however, citizenship for foreign-born Asian people was still a problem. Only immigrants from China, the Philippines, and India were eligible for citizenship. Japanese, Koreans, and other Asian nationalities were not.

Postwar Immigration Law

Meanwhile, in Europe, the government of Germany arrested millions of Jews and other ethnic groups and herded them into death camps. Thousands of desperate Jewish refugees boarded ships for the risky trip to the United States. The U.S. government, fearing that a large number of refugees would cause economic and social problems, turned many of the refugees away.

As the German armies retreated in the spring of 1945, millions of Europeans were driven from their homes. Desperate fighting on the ground and a bombing campaign by the Allies destroyed entire cities. After the final surrender of Germany in May 1945, civilians without homes or jobs fled Europe and came to the United States.

The plight of the Jews and the postwar European refugees changed attitudes about immigration. After World War II,

Congress passed new laws allowing refugees due to military conflict and political persecution to settle in the United States. In 1948 Congress passed the Displaced Persons Act. This allowed a quota of "displaced persons" to enter the country, a total of 200,000.[5] Many of those who arrived were from communist countries in eastern Europe.

Immigration was much easier after the war. After World War II, air travel became easy and cheap. Airline companies set up regular routes to Europe and Latin America. One busy route linked New York City with Puerto Rico. This became the favored way for Puerto Ricans, who were already U.S. citizens, to move north. Large Puerto Rican *barrios,* or neighborhoods, grew in New York.

In the meantime, the national-origins system was coming under fire in Congress. Opinions followed party lines. President Harry Truman and the Democratic Party were against it. Republicans supported it.

In 1952 the McCarran-Walter Act became law. This Act kept the national-origins system of the 1924 law. But the new law allowed citizenship to any and all foreign-born immigrants, even the Asians who were previously excluded. A section of the act known as the Texas Proviso made it unlawful for anyone to harbor (shelter) an illegal alien, although it set no penalties for employers who hired them.

The Displaced Persons Act of 1948 allowed 202,000 nonquota immigrants from communist nations, such as the Soviet Union and the People's Republic of China.[6] The law also admitted anyone forced from home and unable to return. The law included a provision for Asian refugees. In 1956 the law was broadened to include the Middle East and in 1962 Latin America.

> **After World War II, the plight of the Jews and European refugees changed American attitudes about immigration. Congress passed new laws allowing refugees to settle in the United States.**

In the meantime, European and Canadian immigration to the U.S. was declining, and Asian and Latin immigration was increasing. A postwar economic boom was taking place in Europe; while western Europe prospered, the communist nations of eastern Europe did not allow their citizens to leave. Immigration from Mexico increased sharply.

In 1965, the Hart-Celler Act ended the quota limits on individual countries. The law set caps on the yearly number of immigrants from each hemisphere: 170,000 were allowed from the eastern hemisphere (Asia, Africa, and Europe), and 120,000 from the western hemisphere (North and South America). Each country from the eastern hemisphere had a limit of 20,000 immigrants. Refugees became part of the general immigration law. (The Refugee Act of 1980 created the right of asylum for political refugees who had already arrived in the U.S., legally or illegally.)

Under the Hart-Celler Act, legal immigrants, after gaining citizenship, could bring along family members: parents, spouses, siblings, and children. These family members did not count against the quotas. (Also exempt from quotas were laborers in professions that needed workers.) Although the global quota of immigrants was set at 290,000, the actual number of legal immigrants was much greater because of this "chain migration" of family members to the United States. In addition, many countries passed the 20,000-immigrant limit, including Mexico, the Philippines, and Korea.

The law was meant to create a more humane system for immigrants. It had important consequences. Through the late 1960s and the 1970s, it brought a new flood of immigrants from poor countries in Asia, Africa, and Latin America. These newcomers moved into large ethnic neighborhoods, just as the Irish and Italians had lived within urban enclaves in the late nineteenth century. Los Angeles, California, became a huge mosaic of such immigrant neighborhoods, such as Koreatown,

Little Tokyo, and Chinatown. After the Vietnam War, which ended in 1975, refugees flooded into Westminster, a suburb of Los Angeles that became the largest Vietnamese community in the nation.

Immigrants made up significant numbers of people working in construction, restaurants, hotels, and other service industries where wages were relatively low. But the immigrants also raised the cost of public services, such as hospitals and schools. Many people saw the country being divided into unassimilated groups—that is, separate groups that kept their own languages and cultures. Again, native-born Americans grew nervous at the changing ethnic mix of the country. In his book *State of Emergency*, conservative commentator Patrick Buchanan claims the new immigration had the opposite effect of what it had intended:

> The 1965 . . . bill was the greatest bait-and-switch in history. Americans were promised one result, and got the opposite result. . . . They were misled. They were deceived. They were swindled. They were told immigration levels would remain roughly the same and the ethnic composition of their country would not change. What they got was a Third World invasion that is converting America into another country.[8]

The reaction was the same as it had been a century before. Some American citizens saw their way of life and traditions threatened by outsiders. They were certain that immigrants could not, or would not, assimilate into American society.

Dealing with Illegal Immigration

Congress approached the issue of illegal immigration in 1986. In that year, the legislature passed the Immigration Reform and Control Act. Senator Alan Simpson and Representative Romano Mazzoli sponsored the bill. The bill granted temporary residency to those living in the United States without permission since 1982. It also set down penalties for employers who hired illegal aliens. This closed the loophole for employers that had been in place since the Texas Proviso of 1952. Through the Special Agricultural Worker (SAW) program, anyone who worked in agriculture for ninety days in each of three previous years was eligible to become a temporary resident.

There were penalties for knowingly hiring illegal immigrants, including fines and jail time. But enforcement was lax, and the penalties did not stop the hiring of illegal immigrants. Employers were expected to ask for Social Security numbers from their new employees, and to check documents, such as passports, "green cards" (for legal permanent residents), and birth certificates. Most employers simply took it on faith that the documents provided to them were genuine. Many illegal immigrants were able to obtain false Social Security cards in order to open bank accounts, get driver's licenses, and obtain loans.

As foreigners became more visible, voters demanded some action from Congress. At the beginning of the twenty-first century, illegal immigration remained a pressing issue. Political leaders were still trying to come up with sound laws and policy. The immigration debate will continue as long as America attracts newcomers from all over the globe with its promises of freedom and opportunity.

Illegal Immigration

On a hot day in May 2003, an eighteen-wheel semi-trailer truck rolled through the Texas desert. In the back, seventy people from Mexico and Central America were hiding. They had crossed the border of Mexico illegally. Members of a smuggling ring had put them aboard the truck.

The sun burned down, and the temperature in the truck began to rise. The hot air was hard to breathe. There was no water. Some of the stowaways pounded on the walls of the truck, screaming for help. Others began to die.

Tyrone Williams, the truck's driver, pulled into a gas station in Victoria, Texas. He was one hundred miles from his destination.

He heard the pounding and yelling in the back. He opened the doors. Bodies were lying on the floor of the truck. Frightened, Williams ran from the scene.

The police soon captured Williams. He was tried for smuggling illegal aliens into the country. He was also tried for the deaths of nineteen people. For this, he was sentenced to life in prison, without the possibility of parole.

Crossing Without Papers

Illegal immigration has occurred since the late nineteenth century, when many Chinese workers stowed away on ships crossing the Pacific Ocean to the United States. At the start of the twentieth century, stricter controls at U.S. ports slowed illegal immigration. New federal laws kept out most people who did not have permission to enter the U.S. There was no air travel at this time. Automobiles were not common in the southwest, where roads were rare. Ships could be easily stopped and searched in port. Port officials checked the documents of every passenger coming off a ship.

Travel was still difficult for most people in Latin America. Private automobiles and trucks were rare. The northern deserts of Mexico were sparsely inhabited, and a long distance from large cities and fertile valleys farther south.

Later, the American economy began to attract Mexican immigrants. At the same time, the population in both Mexico and the United States became more mobile. Poor farmers from southern Mexican states traveled to the border region, then crossed at night. Once they were settled in the United States, they could host friends and relatives.

By the 1990s, illegal immigration was occurring along every border of the United States, and in port cities and at airports. People were driving and flying into the United States with false visas (official papers attached to passports, which allow entry into the country). They were stowing away on ships and hiding in trucks and vans. Some simply walked across the border in places where there were no fences or barriers.

Illegal immigration across the southern frontier holds many dangers. The region is mostly desert. There are few sources of freshwater. The days are hot, and the nights are cold. Many who try to cross the border there die of heatstroke or dehydration.

Thousands risk the journey anyway. They leave their homes for Mexican towns just south of the border, including Tijuana, Juarez, and Matamoros. They pay "coyotes" (smugglers) hundreds of dollars to guide them into the United States.

The coyotes move at night. They avoid settled areas and roads. They follow a network of trails through the desert. They make camp during the day. They meet vans and pickup trucks on deserted highways.

The drivers carry their passengers into major cities. The illegal immigrants disappear into residential neighborhoods. They stay with friends or family members who have already crossed into the United States. Illegal immigrants can easily fade into the background.

The migration across the border leaves a trail of environmental damage and vandalism. One *Time* magazine article described the scene:

> Night after night, they cut fences intended to hold in cattle and horses. . . . The immigrants steal vehicles . . . [and] poison dogs to quiet them. The illegal traffic is so heavy that some ranchers, because of the disruptions and noise, get very little sleep at night.[1]

The newcomers do not have documents that allow them to work. They do not have work permits or visas that would allow them to stay in the United States and obtain a Social Security number. One purpose of this nine-digit number is to identify legal residents. The Social Security Administration issues the numbers only to people who are in the country legally.

Even without a Social Security number, finding work is not a problem. "Undocumented" aliens will hear of a company or

An agent of U.S. Customs and Border Protection frisks a woman being returned to Mexico after attempting to enter the United States illegally.

an individual, who needs workers. When applying for a job in a store or factory, they can borrow the Social Security number of another person and use it. They can also buy a Social Security number "stolen" from somebody else. The number is used without that person's permission.

To verify the legal status of workers, employers are asked to complete Form I-9, "Employment Eligibility Verification." They must ask for documents proving that the worker is in the country legally. Although most companies will ask for a Social Security number, individuals in need of workers often will not. They do not want to fill out lengthy forms. They simply need help for manual-labor jobs: construction, gardening, maintenance, or repairs. For this "day labor," they meet and gather as many workers as they need. They do not ask for any numbers or documents. At the end of the day, they pay their workers in cash.

Asking for Documents

Operation Southern Denial swung into action in 1998. Fifty agents of the Immigration and Naturalization Service (INS) gathered in Glennville, in southern Georgia. They drove to nearby onion farms. They asked for documents from every worker they saw. They found hundreds of illegal aliens.

The INS agents arrested twenty-nine people. Other workers fled the scene, never to return. The onion farms lost most of their workforce. Unpicked onions were left in the fields to rot.

The onion growers complained about the arrests. They wrote to their representatives in Washington, D.C. The representatives demanded that the government put an end to Operation Southern Denial. They were harming the onion farmers when they needed workers most, at harvest time.

In response, the government announced a "mini-amnesty." The raids would not be repeated. The next year, undocumented workers returned to Georgia to pick the onion crop.

At harvest time, large farms raising fruits and vegetables need workers. They must gather huge crops of tomatoes, onions, oranges, and lettuce. They only have a few weeks to bring in their crops. They cannot manage it with a small permanent workforce. They need temporary seasonal help. They can hire workers who enter the country with H-2A visas. These visas allow people to work for a season, then require them to return to their home country.

To hire temporary workers, the law requires employers to fill out documents stating they need temporary workers. It requires them to pay the federal minimum wage, which rises to $6.55 per hour in 2008 and $7.25 per hour in 2009. (Some states have a higher minimum wage.) To obtain the visas, the workers must fill out application forms and wait for the immigration service to approve their documents.

Many employers and workers do not bother. In California, Florida, Texas, and Washington state, illegal aliens flood into farming areas to work the harvest. Labor costs are an important part of the price of goods, including food. If one farm uses inexpensive, undocumented workers, it lowers its costs and can sell its goods at lower prices. Other farms must do the same, or they will lose money. The undocumented workers cannot demand benefits, such as health insurance. Nor does the employer have to buy workers' compensation insurance to help the workers in case of an accident.

At harvest time, large farms have a few weeks to bring in their crops. They cannot manage it with a small permanent workforce. They need temporary seasonal help.

Large companies working in the food industry use illegal aliens as well. Agents of the Immigration and Customs Enforcement (ICE) department raided the Swift meatpacking plant in Worthington, Minnesota, in December 2006. They arrested 230 people for fraud and for the theft of Social Security numbers. These people were from Mexico, Guatemala, Honduras, Laos, Sudan, Ethiopia, El Salvador, and Peru.

There were simultaneous raids on Swift plants in six other states. More people were arrested for fraud and identity theft. Swift was already taking part in the Basic Pilot program, which helps employers verify their employees' work authorization and find false Social Security numbers. But the company was not identifying stolen numbers to the federal government.

Overstaying the Visa

Not all illegal immigrants sneak across the border. Many students, scientists, businesspeople, tourists, and relatives of legal

Immigration Alphabet Soup

Agencies and terms associated with immigration are often abbreviated, and the names can be confusing. Here are some of the most common ones:

DHS (Department of Homeland Security)—The federal agency charged with protecting the country against terrorism. DHS is now also responsible for enforcing federal immigration law.

H-1B—A visa that allows a skilled foreign worker sponsored by an American employer to come to the United States. Federal law limits the number of H-1B visas that can be issued every year.

ICE (Immigration and Customs Enforcement)—The government agency that investigates immigration violations. ICE is also responsible for securing the country against illegal aliens and foreign terrorists.

INS (Immigration and Naturalization Service)—The agency that at one time handled immigration matters, including the issuance of visas and enforcement. The INS was part of the Department of Justice. It was phased out in 2003.

USA PATRIOT Act (Uniting and Strengthening America by Providing Appropriate Tools Required to Intercept and Obstruct Terrorism)—A federal law passed in October 2001, meant to coordinate and enhance the work of federal agencies responsible for preventing terrorism.

USCIS (United States Citizenship and Immigration Services)—The new immigration agency, part of the Department of Homeland Security, founded after the terrorist attacks of 2001.

US-VISIT (US Visitor and Immigrant Status Indicator Technology)—A system that collects biometric information, such as fingerprints and retina scans, from all foreign visitors at border checkpoints, airports, and other entry points.

immigrants arrive with visas, which represent formal permission from the government to enter U.S. territory. The visa permits a person to stay a certain length of time in the United States. When the visitor arrives—usually at an airport—a U.S. customs official examines the passport, and stamps the visa with the date and location. The date stamp starts the clock on the legal visit. Within a fixed period of time, the visaholder must leave the United States.

Not all visitors pay attention to the law. When their visa expires, some simply remain in the United States. "Overstayers" have the same rights as legal resident aliens. Local police rarely report an illegal alien to the Department of Homeland Security (DHS) or any federal agency. And the ICE does not have the facilities to hold all illegal aliens, or enough workers to examine all their cases and deport them. Unless they are convicted of a crime, illegal immigrants are unlikely to be sent out of the country.

The United States does have a system in place to track legal visitors. Before arriving in the United States, all noncitizens fill out an I-94 form. This is a white card that asks for information: name, date and place of birth, date of entry, and the place where the visitor will stay. At the border, U.S. customs agents stamp the card in two places, and keep a portion of it. The card is sent to a processing center. Foreign arrivals to the United States are also photographed and fingerprinted (as part of the US-VISIT program). The I-94 form is added to a huge database of information known as the Nonimmigrant Information System, or NIIS.

Upon leaving the U.S., the visitor returns the individual portion of the I-94 form. If the person is traveling by air, the airline collects the card. The airline is responsible for turning the cards over to the DHS.

Many of the cards are incomplete or simply missing. Airlines rarely prevent anyone from flying because they do not have

At immigration reform rallies all over the country, immigrants express their feelings about taking part in the American dream.

their I-94 or because the information on the card is wrong. Doing so would slow traffic through airports. This would result in delays, missed flights for other passengers, and problems for the airline.

As a result, the NIIS system has a vast database of almost useless information. It fails to identify thousands of people who arrive legally, but who overstay. It does nothing to enforce visa time limits.

The system sometimes provides valuable information to the police. But the police are responsible for criminal matters, not immigration. In effect, the DHS has no system of catching and deporting people who overstay their visas.

Deportable and Inadmissible

The United States has many federal laws on illegal immigration. Some of the laws date to 1952. In this year, the government set down the procedure for deporting people who should not be in the country. It also gave rules for people who are "inadmissible."

Those who are inadmissible cannot get a visa to enter the United States. Among them are people with more than one criminal conviction, drug traffickers, and those who carry HIV, the virus that can lead to AIDS. People can also be excluded because of their political beliefs. Members of a totalitarian political party, for example, cannot get visas. Former Nazis and war criminals cannot enter the United States.

Some people already in the United States may also be deportable. If they falsified their visa applications, or if they overstay their visas, they can be sent back home. They can also be deported for marriage fraud. Some immigrants come to the United States engaged to be married to an American citizen. In some cases, however, the person arranged the marriage only to win a visa (spouses of American citizens can become legal residents, and then citizens).

Also deportable are those who smuggle others into the

country, are convicted of a serious crime, falsify any official documents, or change their address without notifying the government. By law, anyone deported from the United States within the last five years cannot return.

Since 1952, however, illegal immigrants have arrived and stayed by the millions. By some estimates, there may be 12 million illegals living in the United States.[2] The 1986 Immigration Reform and Control Act allowed amnesty for illegal immigrants in the United States. These immigrants had to have lived in the country continuously since before January 1, 1982.

The Supreme Court decision in the case of *Plyler* v. *Doe* said that schools cannot screen out illegal immigrants or refuse public education to anyone. In border states and Florida, the children of illegal immigrants make up a large percentage of the students. Many of the children are citizens, because they were born in the United States. The cost of public services, such as schools and hospitals, has become a key issue in the debate on illegal immigration.

Proposition 187

Illegal immigration first became a serious problem in California. Like all states, California maintains a public school system. It requires all children under a certain age to attend school. The state also supports public hospitals and has a system of benefits for poor and unemployed people.

Illegal immigrants use these systems. As more undocumented workers arrive, more of them use schools and hospitals. These public services grow more crowded and more costly. California has often raised taxes to keep its schools and agencies open. But the state does not have enough money in its treasury to fund them. To avoid a budget crisis, it must raise taxes or close down public services.

Many people resist any rise in taxes. In 1994, voters in California reacted to illegal immigration with Proposition 187.

This ballot initiative was intended to change state law by popular vote. Proposition 187 required all those applying for public benefits to prove they were citizens or legal residents.

Proposition 187 also would have required police to investigate anyone suspected of being illegal. If police found an illegal immigrant, they would have to report that immigrant to the INS (now the USCIS) and to the attorney general of California for possible deportation.

The initiative inspired angry protest. Latinos in California felt the law targeted them. They saw Proposition 187 as unfair and unconstitutional. On October 15, 1994, more than 100,000 people marched through downtown Los Angeles in protest. But on November 8, 1994, Proposition 187 passed by a large majority—59 percent of the vote.

Opponents of the law appealed to the courts. According to their argument, only the federal government can make laws concerning the rights of immigrants, legal or illegal. Opponents also argued against the law-enforcement rules. They saw them as violating the constitutional right of "equal protection." According to this principle, everyone—no matter their race, color, creed, or citizenship status—must be treated equally in the courts and by the police.

As illegal immigrants use public schools, hospitals, and other institutions, these services grow more crowded and more costly. States must raise taxes or close down services.

Judges struck down the new laws. Proposition 187 never went into effect. In many other locales, similar laws have been challenged in the courts. Yet the budget crisis in California, and in many other cities and states, still inspires similar laws. Proposition 200 passed in Arizona in 2004. This law requires all those registering to vote, or applying for public benefits such as welfare, to prove they are citizens. Many people protested Proposition 200, and the state's governor and senators opposed it as well. Despite court challenges, Proposition 200 remains valid law in Arizona.

Bilingualism

In 1998 California passed another ballot initiative, known as Proposition 227. This law instructed all public schools to teach only in English. Proposition 227 was a reaction to the trend toward bilingual education. Beginning in the 1970s, many cities passed new rules for their public schools. These rules stated that children unable to speak English had to be instructed in their native languages.

Demonstrators opposed to illegal immigration protest in Tucson, Arizona. The immigration debate stirs strong feelings on all sides.

The rules were intended to help young immigrants who could not understand English. The bilingual education plan was simple. Young immigrants would learn temporarily in their native languages. At the same time, the students would learn English. Eventually, they would join bilingual classes, where students used both languages.

Bilingual education, however, did not go as planned. Many schools made instruction in the foreign language permanent. Many students learned in Spanish, or Vietnamese, or Hindi, and were slow to learn English. And because qualified, native speakers of some languages were hard to find, schools hired teachers from foreign countries to teach bilingual classes. Some of these teachers were not fluent in English and neglected English-language instruction.

As a result, some "bilingual" students left school with a limited ability to speak English. They were at a disadvantage in applying for college or even finding a job. The education system had not met a basic need—preparation for survival in their new country.

Herman Badillo, a politician from New York, grew up speaking Spanish in a Puerto Rican neighborhood of New York City. He was an enthusiastic supporter of bilingual education. He played a leading role in getting the city to adopt it. Eventually, however, he had a change of heart. Nevertheless, bilingual education remains an important policy within the New York City school system. In his book, *One Nation, One Standard*, Badillo expresses this view on the subject:

> We are and have been one nation, with one standard, which has been that regardless of what part of the world we may have originated from, we came here to strengthen and reinforce the culture and traditions of this country. Above all, we must be prepared to learn the English language as fast as possible so that we can be full participants in this society.[3]

Illegal immigration increased in the 1990s. Congress reacted with the Illegal Immigration Reform and Immigrant Responsibility Act. This law targeted illegal immigrants. They were excluded from Social Security and Medicare benefits, even if they paid into these programs. They could be deported for offenses committed before the passage of the law, even if they had paid fines and/or served prison sentences. Anyone convicted of a crime and sentenced to a year or more in prison was subject to immediate deportation.

The law covered legal immigrants and permanent residents as well. Anyone convicted of a crime could be deported from the country permanently. They could be held in a detention center until their case is heard. It does not matter how long the immigrant has lived in the United States. Many legal residents have been separated from their families and sent back to countries where they have no friends, families, jobs, or opportunity.

Some provisions of the law were repealed within a few years. But the debate on illegal immigration continued. The economic costs of illegal immigration lay at the heart of the debate. Some believe that immigrants are a heavy expense; others believe that they bring economic benefits. The debate over the cost of immigration is part of a larger question: the future of the country in a "global" economy, in which goods and people move more freely from one country and continent to another. For the United States, prospering in this new era of globalism depends on a smart immigration policy.

Immigration and the U.S. Economy

4

Do immigrants cost society more than they produce? Lawmakers, historians, teachers, and politicians still debate this question. At one time, the immigration debate was about ethnic origins. Ethnicity is still an important part of immigration issues. But the real controversy surrounds the economic costs associated with immigrants.

Many believe immigration benefits the United States economy. They believe that immigrants contribute more than their share to business and the public treasury. Others point out the high price of providing services, such as education and health care, to new arrivals. They also worry about immigrants driving down wages. Undocumented workers may not demand decent wages or benefits. When immigrants accept low pay for work in a factory or farm, other businesses may also lower their wages in order to compete.

Many companies depend on the labor of immigrants. They have a problem finding U.S. citizens willing to do certain jobs. They will bend the rules in order to hire willing workers. In the meantime, the government tries to enforce immigration law and catch illegal aliens. A showdown between government and private business is the result.

Operation Vanguard

One of the largest INS enforcement operations took place in 1999. Operation Vanguard, also known as Operation Prime Beef, took place in Nebraska, Iowa, and South Dakota. One of its targets was IBP, a company that operates large meatpacking plants in Lexington, Nebraska. INS agents arrived in Lexington and demanded the company turn over all of its I-9 forms.

The I-9 form lists data on everyone hired by the company. The worker provides a name and a document, usually either a Social Security number or a work permit. The INS can compare the Social Security numbers with those on record at the Social Security Administration. If the name and the number do not seem to match, an investigation starts.

Lawmakers, historians, teachers, and politicians still debate this question: Do immigrants cost U.S. society more than they produce?

After the IBP raid, the INS found 318 instances in which the names and Social Security numbers did not match those on record. After checking the numbers, INS agents returned to the Lexington plant. By then, 185 of the workers had quit. Of those who remained, one was arrested, one was fired, eight did not show up for work, seventeen had an excused absence from work, and 106 were allowed to remain as legal workers.[1]

The action drove away many workers fearing deportation. Work at the plants slowed. Because the plants worked slower, they did not purchase as much livestock from farmers. As demand for meat went down, so did the price.

Employers, farmers, and members of Congress protested Operation Vanguard. The operation came to a halt. The IBP plants returned to full capacity, with managers promising to be more careful about immigration documents.

The IBP raid highlighted the economic debate between labor and business owners over immigration. "Legal" workers generally seek stricter limits on immigration, while many business owners want more open borders and a more tolerant policy. When writing immigration law, the Congress tries to strike a balance. The federal government tries to set a reasonable limit on the number of visas it grants every year. It also wants to encourage immigrants to become residents, productive workers, and eventually citizens.

Under certain circumstances, the United States allows "guest workers" to immigrate. These are temporary foreign employees hired by private companies. They are granted visas for a limited period of time. When the time expires, they must leave the country. The first such guest-worker program began in the southwestern United States. It was a time of war, and the necessary workers were extremely scarce.

The Bracero Program

The United States is the global leader in agriculture. There is plenty of land, growing seasons are long, and rainfall in most of the country is abundant. In dry climates, irrigation brings freshwater to the fields. As a result of these conditions, the market price of fruit, grain, vegetables, and meat holds steady. Another result is that farmworkers, ranch hands, and harvesting crews do not earn very much.

Young people give up farming and leave rural areas for better opportunity in the cities. The farms they leave behind still need workers. During World War II, the farm labor shortage worsened, especially in the southwest. In 1942, the United States invited workers from Mexico to come north and help. The first Mexican *braceros* ("laborers") picked sugar beets near Stockton, California.

The braceros were paid low wages. But they were making much more than they could in Mexico. The program was supposed to benefit workers by forcing them to save money. The growers who employed the braceros were supposed to send some of the pay to their workers' savings accounts in Mexico.

The program spread to the transportation sector, which also needed workers. Railroad braceros maintained track. Altogether, there were more than 100,000 braceros working in the United States at the end of World War II.

In the meantime, illegal immigrants were still making their way north from Mexico. Author Michael Barone describes a scene long familiar along the Rio Grande River:

> People would cross the river into the Lower Rio Grande Valley to work in Texas fields during the day and then return to their homes in Mexico at night, or they might live in Texas; no one outside the area much cared, for there was no mass migration any farther north.[2]

Problems developed in the bracero program. The workers lived in poor housing. Growers imposed bad working conditions. Money sent to the immigrants' bank accounts in Mexico was disappearing. The problems caused a scandal when media reported them.

In 1964, the U.S. government ended the bracero program. The growers using the guest workers protested, claiming they could not survive without bracero labor. But, unexpectedly, the growers thrived after losing their guest workers. Tomato growers, for example, were forced to develop machinery to pick their

Former migrant workers demonstrate in Mexico. Part of the bracero program, they lost money when the pay they sent home disappeared at a Mexican bank.

crops. This mechanization made their operations more efficient and profitable.

In addition, workers continued to arrive from Mexico to work the harvest. Some were legal guest workers, some were not. The bracero program had begun an important system of migrant, seasonal labor in the southwest. Farms needed workers, and Mexican workers sought jobs. There was demand for more immigration on both sides of the border.

Guest Workers

The United States still issues a guest-worker visa for farm laborers, the H-2A. But the program is often ignored. Many workers and employers avoid the cumbersome process of filling out forms and waiting for the government to issue working papers. Illegal immigrants arrive to work harvests all over the country, and many of them live permanently in the United States.

In the meantime, President George W. Bush proposed expanding the guest-worker program to grant legal status to millions of undocumented aliens. Many people, on both sides of the immigration debate, are opposed to this plan. Farmworkers do not want to see increased competition and a fall in their wages. Those favoring tight controls on immigration also believe a guest-worker program is a bad idea. They predict it will lead to a flood of new illegal immigrants across the border. In 2007, the plan was defeated in the U.S. Congress.

Some economists point out that using humans to pick crops will soon be a thing of the past. In Japan and Europe, some farms are now using robotic harvesters. Because the cost of labor in these regions is high, using robots makes economic sense. But in the United States, investment in robotic harvesting is unnecessary as long as cheap human labor is available. If no new investment in technology is made, however, American farms are in danger of falling behind their competitors.

Working Off the Books

A large percentage of legal immigrants are in low-wage occupations. Nineteen percent of these immigrants work in service industries, 19 percent in retail trade, 15 percent in manufacturing, and 9 percent in construction.[3]

Many illegal immigrants work for decent wages, earn some benefits, and pay the same taxes as legal workers. But many of them—especially undocumented workers without English language skills—will work for less money than citizens. They have very limited ability to demand better wages. They do not want it known they are illegally employed, so many will work "off the books," with no record of their hiring. They do not receive any benefits, such as health insurance. In some industries, insurance is almost as great a cost to the employer as salaries.

Casual workers, who work for cash and for a limited time, almost always work off the books. They do not draw regular paychecks, and they do not pay any taxes. Many gardeners, for example, are hired by the day and paid at the end of the day. Some maintenance workers, nannies, maids, mechanics, repair workers, and couriers do not have identity papers or Social Security numbers and are paid in cash. Many taxi drivers also operate independently. They are not paid a salary. In effect, they rent their cabs from taxi companies and work for themselves. In most large cities, many cabdrivers are immigrants, and some are undocumented.

An employer hiring a casual laborer can also avoid paying workers' compensation insurance (workers' comp). This guarantees medical care for a worker who is injured on the job. Most states require companies to have workers' comp. But they only require it for regular, salaried workers. Anyone working off the books does not have this protection. If they should get hurt while working, they must pay for their own health care. If they protest to the employer, the employer can easily retaliate—by reporting their illegal status to the authorities.

The effect of this underground economy is to depress wages for legal workers. Hardest hit are those at the lower ends of wage scale. Low-wage workers compete with illegal immigrants for jobs. But immigrants—even illegal immigrants—provide benefits to the economy in certain ways. They take on jobs that people with education and training will not do. Restaurants, hotels, farms, clothing and textile factories, and food processing industries rely heavily on unskilled workers. Without them, the companies could not remain open and compete with foreign firms that pay their workers even less. Jobs would become scarcer for everyone.

In addition, immigrants rent apartments and homes, and

they buy things, providing a market for goods and services. They also remit (send) money to families in their home countries. These remittances are an important source of income in Mexico and other countries. In poor towns and rural areas they provide families with a better standard of living. By doing this, remittances may deter even more illegal immigration.

Foreign-born workers with regular paychecks must also pay into the Social Security system. This federal program provides benefits to retirees and to those unable to work, such as the disabled. If they do not become citizens, these immigrants cannot draw out Social Security benefits. The Social Security system will keep the taxes they paid without reimbursing them.

A man works on a roof in the hot sun. People argue that those who enter the country illegally and are hired as day laborers depress wages for legal workers.

As immigrants move up the economic ladder, their contribution increases in value. As business owners, they create jobs as well. In addition, they tend to rely less on public services and welfare (government benefits to help the poor). Their salaries increase, they pay more taxes, and they consume more goods and services. "Second generation" Americans usually do better than their parents. They are citizens by right of birth, and most of them join the economic mainstream. Their skills and experience benefit the country by making the economy more productive.

Closed or Open Borders?

The number of immigrants to the U.S. increased at the end of the twentieth century. One immigration study explains:

> According to the 1990 census, roughly one in twelve residents of the United States was born abroad. In some states, such as California, Florida, and Texas, nearly one in four residents is an immigrant. It is estimated that there are more people of Polish descent living in the United States than in Poland.[4]

Immigration was nearly as high in the 1980s and 1990s as it was in the first decade of the twentieth century, when 15 percent of the population was foreign-born—an all-time record.[5] The recent wave of immigration has inspired opponents of "open borders." They believe immigrants are no longer vital to the economy. At one time, the United States needed a large pool of laborers to build cities, farms, and transportation networks. Now that the United States makes more from service businesses than from manufacturing, mining, and farming (combined), low-skilled workers are more of a burden on the society than an economic benefit, or so these opponents of immigration claim.

The reverse argument, however, is a strong one. Legal immigrants tend to be business entrepreneurs. They start up their own businesses, and work hard to survive. Their success creates more jobs and contributes to economic growth.

The United States benefits greatly from skilled foreign labor. This includes nurses, teachers, carpenters, electricians, computer programmers, software designers, mechanics, and doctors. In industries that build robots, computers, and semiconductors, foreign engineers are crucial. If these skilled workers cannot come to the United States, they will stay home or go elsewhere, helping foreign companies compete against the United States.

There are other reasons for welcoming immigrants. Different cultures contribute to the "melting pot" and the vitality of American life. New ideas arrive with foreign teachers, artists, and writers. Immigrants who move into urban areas stabilize their neighborhoods. Many urban precincts in the United States would be nearly empty without immigrants who live, work, and pay taxes there.

Some people favor an increase in immigration. They point out some important trends that will occur in the twenty-first century. The large generation of "baby boomers," born from

> **Immigration was nearly as high in the 1980s and 1990s as it was in the first decade of the twentieth century, when 15 percent of the population was foreign-born—an all-time record.**

1946 to 1964, will retire. Birthrates among the native-born population of the United States are in decline. The number of new workers is also declining. The federal government, taking in fewer taxes, will be hard-pressed to provide Medicare and Social Security benefits to retirees. For this reason, many people see increased immigration as a way to keep the U.S. economy working at full steam, and holding its place as the largest in the world.

No matter which side of the debate, most people agree that the law on immigration is too complex. The federal regulations covering immigration fill thick books with fine print. There are dozens of different visas, each with its own set of rules, deadlines, and restrictions.

To make matters worse, the federal government does not have enough workers to process and approve visa applications. The system is slow and bewildering, and there is no easy way of changing it. Applying for a visa will always be difficult until the government hires more agents and speeds up the system. That is an important reason millions of immigrants are simply cheating the system, sneaking across the border or overstaying their visas, and living in the United States as illegal aliens.

Visas and Citizenship

The United States has very complex immigration laws. Immigrants must navigate a maze of applications, rules, fees, deadlines, and penalties. They must provide photographs, documents, and sworn statements to support their applications. In theory, immigration laws allow the government to control what kinds of visitors cross its borders and who can stay. In practice, the system frustrates desirable immigrants and prompts others to simply go around the law.

Visas fall into two categories: immigrant and nonimmigrant. The nonimmigrant visas are for people who only wish to stay in the United States temporarily. These include students (who apply for an F visa), journalists (the I visa), and tourists (the B-2 visa). Another very important nonimmigrant visa is for workers: the H-1B. This visa attracts more attention than most others, both in the United States and in foreign countries.

Working Immigrants

The H-1B visa was designed in 1989 for skilled workers. But anyone with specialized knowledge or training can apply for this visa. Doctors, lawyers, accountants, engineers, business owners, and fashion models all may apply for the H-1B.

The law currently sets a limit of 65,000 H-1B visas to be issued every year. A total of 20,000 additional H-1B visas are reserved for foreigners who hold advanced degrees from U.S. universities.[1] The quotas begin to run with visa applications received on October 1. Every year, the U.S. Congress reviews this quota number. It can change the quota to meet demand.

Visitors holding an H-1B visa can stay in the United States for up to three years. Their visas can be renewed one time, for another three years. H-1B visaholders may also apply to become permanent residents.

The H-1B visa allows the United States to bring new, skilled people into its workforce. These people help American companies compete with foreign companies. Some people criticize the H-1B visa, however, and believe issuing these visas is a bad idea. They believe that some companies are hiring foreign workers and using them to replace American workers, although this is against the law.

There are several other kinds of temporary work visas. The O-1 visa is for those with a special ability. They may be artists, musicians, athletes, scientists, writers, or educators. A rock group from Europe, for example, travels on an O visa. Tennis players and golfers get O visas to play in tournaments in the U.S.

The L-1 visa is for a U.S. company that does business in

a foreign country. The company may want to bring one of its foreign managers or engineers to the United States. The employee may train people or work on a project. The rules state that the foreign employee must work for the company in a foreign country for at least a year before coming to the United States. People who hold L-1 visas may also apply to become permanent residents in the United States.

Family Visas

There are also immigrant visas for family members of U.S. citizens. These K visas are for parents, children, spouses, or other members of the family. There are no quota limits set on K visas.

An immigrant may also come to the United States to marry a U.S. citizen. He or she must apply for the K-1 visa. The U.S. citizen petitions for the visa. If the petition is approved, then the immigrant has an interview at the U.S. consulate in the foreign country and has a medical exam.

The K-1 is a nonimmigrant visa. Anyone arriving on this visa has ninety days to get married. If they do not, they become an illegal immigrant and must return to their home country. After the marriage, the new spouse can apply for a "green card," which gives the status of permanent resident. After a waiting period, the new spouse can then apply for citizenship.

The spouse of an American citizen can apply for a K-3 visa and is allowed to bring their children into the country on a K-4 visa. Parents and siblings of U.S. citizens can also come to the United States and apply to become permanent residents. If they are already in the United States on a temporary visa, they can adjust their status. They can become permanent residents, and they can work legally.

Green Cards

There are many different visas for visitors to the United States. But there is only one document for those who wish to stay: the

Permanent Resident Card, or I-551. This is a small plastic card, much like a driver's license or a credit card. It carries a photograph of the bearer, along with name, date of birth, sex, and country of origin.

The I-551 allows a "resident alien" to stay permanently, to apply for citizenship, or to simply stay as long as desired. A resident alien may leave the country at any time, and return without a visa. In the meantime, the holder has the right to work, and the obligation to pay taxes. By law, the I-551 holder

A family from Cali, Colombia, celebrates at a birthday party. By law, all children born in the United States are U.S. citizens, regardless of the immigration status of their parents.

must also carry the card at all times. U.S. citizens are not required to carry identification.

At one time, the I-551 document was printed on green paper. For that reason, people still call the Permanent Resident Card a "green card." The U.S. government issues green cards only to legal immigrants. They must apply for the card, and they must enter the United States on a visa that permits immigration. Most green cards are issued to people who are already in the United States and who apply for an adjustment in their status, from temporary to permanent.

The United States has set up a green-card lottery. About fifty thousand green cards are granted to people from countries where immigration to the United States is low. Anyone selected in this Diversity Lottery Program may bring a spouse and children under the age of twenty-one.

Helping Victims of Crime

At one time, the law required anyone applying for a green card to have a sponsor. The sponsor had to be a citizen or permanent resident. It could be a spouse, a member of the immigrant's family, or a family friend.

In some cases, however, immigrants were victims of abuse within their home. They depended completely on their spouse for survival. They lived under the threat of being forced to return to their native country. The Violence Against Women Act of 1994 changed this sponsorship law. Under this law, spouses who are the victim of domestic violence can "self-petition" for residency. In 2000, the Victims of Trafficking and Violence Protection Act extended this law. This law provided for two new classes of visa. A T visa is granted to someone who is the victim of human trafficking, such as a young woman sold into prostitution. T visas are also for people brought to the United States through fraud and forcibly made to work.

The proposed U visa is a more general category. It would

cover people who are the victims of a crime and who are helping a criminal investigation in the United States. As of 2008, the U visa was still just an idea.

Naturalization

Becoming a citizen is known as "naturalization." To be naturalized, an immigrant must understand the English language, have lived in the United States for at least five years (at least three years for a spouse), and not have a criminal record. The immigrant must not be a member of a communist party or any "totalitarian organization." Former members of Germany's Nazi party, for example, may not become U.S. citizens.

The government makes some exceptions. Anyone who has contributed to national security—meaning a foreign agent of the Central Intelligence Agency (CIA) or another federal agency—may apply for citizenship after only one year of residency.

A resident seeking to become a citizen must fill out the N-400 "Application to File Petition for Naturalization." The USCIS then carries out a background check. The background check verifies the applicant's place of residence, work history, and police record.

After the background check, applicants take a citizenship test. The exam tests their ability in English and their knowledge of American history and government. The USCIS selects questions from a list of 100, which may include:

How many stars are in the flag?

What is the 4th of July?

What is the executive branch of our government?

Who is the current governor of your state?

The applicant who passes the test attends a citizenship ceremony. At the ceremony, the applicant renounces any allegiance to a foreign government, and recites the following oath:

I hereby declare, on oath, that I absolutely and entirely renounce and abjure all allegiance and fidelity to any foreign prince, potentate, state, or sovereignty of whom or which I have heretofore been a subject or citizen; that I will support and defend the Constitution and laws of the United States of America against all enemies, foreign and domestic; that I will bear true faith and allegiance to the same; that I will bear arms on behalf of the United States when required by law; that I will perform noncombatant service in the armed forces of the United States when required by the law; that I will perform work of national importance under civilian direction when required by the law; and that I take this obligation freely without any mental reservation or purpose of evasion; so help me God.[2]

Dual Citizenship—Dual Loyalties?

It is possible to be a citizen of the United States and another country at the same time. The laws covering dual citizenship are complicated. If two U.S. citizens live abroad and have a child, that child may or may not be a citizen. It depends on how long the parents lived in the United States prior to the birth. It is also possible for a U.S. citizen to become the citizen of another country.

Citizens who move abroad remain citizens for as long as they want. They do not have to renounce (give up) their citizenship. The government makes a few exceptions. If a citizen serves in a hostile army, or takes a high position in a foreign government, then the U.S. Department of State can revoke their citizenship.

Dual citizenship can be a problem for immigrants. Their former country may demand that they pay taxes, although they live and work in the United States. Their government may forbid them to travel to certain countries (including the United States). Dual citizens may also be called up for military service. Many countries still have a military draft, and require all young men to serve for a year or two. It is possible for a dual citizen to

Would You Pass the Citizenship Test?

The following are some of the questions used for the U.S. citizenship test. When an immigrant applies for citizenship, he or she must write out the answers to ten questions selected at random from a list of one hundred questions. An applicant passes with a score of 7 or 8, depending on the office where the test is taken. How would you do?

1. What country did we fight during the Revolutionary War?
2. What are the three branches of our government?
3. What are the duties of Congress?
4. Who becomes President of the United States if the President and the vice president should die?
5. Who said, "Give me liberty or give me death"?
6. How many terms can the President serve?
7. Who was Martin Luther King, Jr.?
8. How many Supreme Court justices are there?
9. Why did the Pilgrims come to America?
10. What is the national anthem of the United States?

Answers

1. England
2. Legislative, executive, and judiciary
3. To make laws
4. Speaker of the House of Representatives
5. Patrick Henry
6. Two
7. A civil rights leader
8. Nine (9)
9. For religious freedom
10. "The Star-Spangled Banner"

This citizenship test is going to be replaced by a new test in October 2008. The new test is designed to ask more meaningful questions about the United States.

be legally required to fight in two different armies at the same time.

Many countries have no problem with dual citizenship. In fact, they encourage it. Many Latin American nations, such as Peru and Colombia, see dual citizenship as an advantage. If their emigrants remain citizens, they will keep close ties and allegiance to their home country. But some people see dual citizenship as a problem for the United States. By this argument, a new citizen

> To be naturalized, an immigrant must understand English, have lived in the U.S. for at least five years (at least three years for a spouse), and not have a criminal record.

should cut ties with the former home country and more fully assimilate in the society and culture of the United States. This was the pattern for immigrants in the early twentieth century.

Dual citizenship, and better communication and transportation, led to a change in immigration in the late twentieth century. In many American neighborhoods, entire communities simply transplanted themselves. In his book *Who Are We?*, political scientist Samuel Huntington describes one of these modern "transnational villages":

> Two thirds of the families in Miraflores in the Dominican Republic (a village of four thousand) have relatives in the Boston area. They dominate one neighborhood in the Jamaica Plain area of Boston. . . . The interactions between Miraflores South and Miraflores North are intense and sustained.[3]

There are many more transnational villages. About one half of the former inhabitants of Chinantla, Mexico, now live in New York City. A similar percentage of Casa Blanca, Mexico, has moved to Tulsa, Oklahoma. Intipuca, El Salvador, has transplanted itself to Washington, D.C., and more than 1,000 people have moved from Villachuato, Mexico, to Marshalltown, Iowa, where immigrants make up the majority of workers in a Swift and Company meatpacking plant.

These two-country communities tend to keep their traditional customs and culture. They form development clubs (*clubes de oriundos*) to start new businesses and build homes in their "source country." Their members can easily travel between the two countries. They have less motivation, or need, to blend into the American melting pot.

Waiving the Visa

In recent years the legal immigration system has grown larger, and much slower. It can take many months for foreigners to get an ordinary visa for travel, study, or work. In the meantime, people must deal with an overburdened, inefficient system. The result is impatience, frustration, and ill will between the United States and foreign nations.

New citizens take the oath of allegiance at a naturalization ceremony in Arizona.

The Visa Waiver Program (VWP) is supposed to help. This program began in 1986. It allows citizens of some foreign countries to come to the United States for ninety days without a visa. There are twenty-seven countries in the program, including most of western Europe, Australia, as well as New Zealand, and the Asian nations of Japan, Singapore, and Brunei.[4]

Those who enter the United States on the VWP must have passports. They also must have a return ticket. They must come only as a tourist or on a business trip. They cannot work or apply to become a permanent resident.

The program has come under criticism since the terrorist attacks of 9/11. Many people fear that the VWP allows terrorists an easy way to get onto U.S. soil. Some believe the United States should use the program to reward its allies in the fight against terrorism. Terrorism and other security issues have become a major part in the debate over immigration.

A Threat to the United States?

September 11, 2001, was a busy, normal Tuesday morning. Passengers rushed through security checkpoints at airports all over the country. They passed their luggage through X-ray machines. They presented boarding passes at the gates.

There were thousands of flights preparing for takeoff within the United States. At the boarding gates, nobody demanded passports or did any background checks. There seemed no special need. There were too few airline and security employees, anyway, and too many people hurrying to their planes.

Nineteen of these passengers boarded jets in Boston and Washington, D.C. Soon after takeoff, they hijacked the planes.

Three planes were flown deliberately into the World Trade Center towers in New York City and the Pentagon in Washington. The fourth crashed in a Pennsylvania field.

None of the hijackers were U.S. citizens. Fifteen of them were from Saudi Arabia, one was from Egypt, one was from Lebanon, and two were from the United Arab Emirates. Most were traveling on tourist visas and were in the country legally.

One of the hijackers was Mohammed Atta, an Egyptian. Atta was traveling on a tourist visa. He remained in the U.S. while applying for a student visa, which would have allowed him to stay longer. Although he had once overstayed a visa, he had been granted his tourist visa and was allowed back into the United States. One year after his death, the immigration authorities sent him a letter, granting his change in status.

Preventing Another 9/11

The terrorist attacks of 9/11 caused an immigration crisis. Lawmakers demanded strict limits on immigration and better security. They pointed out the fact that most of the 9/11 terrorists had entered the country legally. They claimed that terrorists could also enter the country illegally, by crossing the long borders with Mexico or Canada. The immigration authorities stepped up deportation of people in the country illegally. In 2000, 108,249 people were deported from the U.S. In 2006, the number had risen to 192,838.[1] The deportations broke up thousands of families and forced many working people, who had come to the United States without a visa, out of the country permanently.

The 9/11 hijackings had not been stopped by the many different systems the government uses for finding and following terrorists. These include computer databases used by the Customs Service, by the Border Patrol, by the FBI, and by other law-enforcement agencies. These databases are simply long lists of names and information. Customs officials, members of the

Border Patrol, and local police can log into some of these systems. They can enter a name; the system looks for a match.

The databases include names, photographs, and information. There is a database for those caught with stolen passports, those who have been deported from the United States, those who have overstayed visas, and those who have been denied visas. The United States also keeps lists of terrorist organizations and their members. This information is collected from police reports, FBI and CIA investigations, the military, and foreign governments and police agencies.

Since the attacks of September 2001, the government has added biometric information to some of its systems. Biometric information includes fingerprints, retina scans (of the eye), and other information that is unique to each individual. The US-VISIT (US Visitor and Immigrant Status Indicator Technology) program collects this information from every foreign visitor who enters the United States. This information is much better at identifying people than document data such as names, birthdates, addresses, and Social Security numbers.

One example of a text-based system is NAILS, the National Automated Immigration Lookout System. Officials at all ports of entry—airports, border posts, harbors—can access this system. It contains information on millions of people, including all foreigners who have applied for visas. The database displays basic biographical information, including criminal history.

Immigration officials use the NAILS database to run background checks on everyone who applies for entry to the United States. They can find out who was granted a visa in the past, and who was rejected, and for what reason.

The NAILS system, however, relies on names, not biometric information. Someone applying for a visa may or may not give a real name. Unless an alias is known to law enforcement, NAILS cannot detect false identities. For this reason, its usefulness in tracking terrorists is very limited.

Workers in the rubble of the former World Trade Center in New York. Following the attacks of September 11, 2001, Americans demanded stricter controls on immigration.

The U.S. Department of State has its own screening and lookout systems. The CLASS (Consular Lookout and Support System) runs background checks for nonimmigrant visas. This system contains information on known terrorists, drug traffickers, and other undesirable aliens. TIPOFF is another system that contains the names of known terrorists. The TIPOFF database is shared with NAILS. Information on the terrorists can be entered into the system through U.S. consulates abroad.

TECS is the Treasury Enforcement Communication System, run by the Customs Service. It tracks criminal suspects. It includes a record of arrest warrants, which the police use to arrest criminal suspects. TECS also has records on stolen vehicles and on vehicles used in the commission of a crime. IBIS (Interagency Border Inspection System) has records related to law enforcement—stolen vehicles or other property, arrest warrants, illegal aliens, stolen passports, visa violations, and criminal histories. It has information collected from the Customs Service, the Department of State, the FBI, and immigration agencies. It can also link to an FBI system known as the National Crime Information Center.

Finally, the APIS (Advance Passenger Information System) is used to screen airline passengers. This program began operating in 1988. At that time it was voluntary—airline companies could use it, or not, as they saw fit. When a passenger in a foreign country arrives for boarding a flight to the United States, the airline checks the APIS system for those with criminal records or who are suspected terrorists. In theory, people with criminal records can be denied passage to the United States. After 9/11, the United States government required use of the APIS system.

Sharing Information

There is one serious flaw in these information systems. Some can be shared, while others cannot. Many different databases exist because each government agency jealously guards its assigned tasks—its "turf." These agencies, such as the FBI and the CIA, do not like to share their information with the public, with the press, or with other agencies. They feel that this information should be kept secret.

Revealing the name of a suspected criminal, for example, might jeopardize an attempt to find and arrest that suspect. Sharing data might also reveal investigative methods and the agency's sources of information. Each government agency claims the right to use the information it collects in the most useful manner. This does not always include giving the information to an outsider who requests it.

Many government agencies, such as the FBI and the CIA, do not like to share their information with the public, the press, or other agencies. They feel that it should be kept secret.

The USA PATRIOT Act was passed in October 2001, six weeks after the terrorist attacks of September 11. USA PATRIOT stands for Uniting and Strengthening America by Providing Appropriate Tools Required to Intercept and Obstruct Terrorism. (Now it is known simply as the Patriot Act.) A Vietnamese immigrant, Assistant Attorney General Viet Dinh, wrote much of the law.

The Patriot Act expanded the government's powers to arrest and detain immigrants. It allowed the government to detain immigrants indefinitely, without charging them. People who were detained had no right to communicate with anyone.

In 2002 the U.S. government mandated that male visitors on temporary visas from thirty-three countries would have to register with their local police, and be fingerprinted and photographed. About 82,000 men complied with this rule, and as a result 13,000 were deported from the country, most because they were "out of status" with the INS with another visa application pending. Of course, terrorists wishing to evade detection did not comply. Several thousand people from the suspect countries simply fled the United States rather than risk detention.

The Patriot Act was opposed by several cities that did not want their police to become immigration enforcers. The Bush administration threatened to withhold federal funds from these "sanctuary cities." This threat was ended by an act of Congress.

The Patriot Act was supposed to solve the government's information problem. The new law gave immigration officials access to FBI files. It also linked several of the existing databases and allowed them to be more widely used.

But not all government databases have been combined. And the computer systems they run on do not always work. Border agents are hard-pressed to process long lines of visitors at airports and road crossings. If their computer systems go down, they cannot send people home or make them wait. For this reason, they often do not run required background checks or examine watch lists.

Border Barriers

San Diego, California, had a serious problem in the early 1990s. The city lies near the U.S.-Mexico border, just north of the cities of Tijuana and Tecate. Busy streets run along the border, and a major freeway, Interstate 5, ends at a crowded international crossing. The San Ysidro checkpoint, at the westernmost point of the U.S.-Mexican border, is the site of a round-the-clock traffic jam. It is the busiest land entry point in the United States.

The U.S. Border Patrol designated sixty-six miles of border as the San Diego Sector. The sector became a magnet for illegal border crossers. It had the highest rate of arrests of illegal immigrants in the entire country. To get into the United States, thousands of people simply jumped a fence. They walked into San Diego without interference.

Although easy, the crossing could also be dangerous. Many people were killed by vehicles while walking along or crossing the freeways and busy roads. There were other problems. One of the most serious was a steeply rising crime rate in neighborhoods adjoining the border. The crimes included assaults, burglaries, rapes, and robberies.

To deal with the problems, the federal government launched Operation Gatekeeper in 1994. Border Patrol agents were given new equipment, such as infrared sensors, to detect people crossing the border illegally. A wall 14 miles long was raised along the border. The wall was made of corrugated steel, reinforced with concrete pillars that prevented cars and vans from simply crashing through the barrier.

The U.S.-Mexico border (the United States is on the left side of the photo). Operation Gatekeeper was launched by the U.S. government in 1994 to deal with those crossing the border illegally.

As a result of Operation Gatekeeper, illegal border crossings at San Ysidro and in the city of San Diego declined. Smugglers and illegal immigrants then moved east, into the Otay Mountains and to remote desert areas east of San Diego. The number of illegal immigrants did not decrease.

Border walls then went up in California, Arizona, and Texas. Many of them are made of surplus steel acquired from the military. They were raised in areas of heavy border traffic, such as the crossing between Ciudad Juarez, Mexico, and El Paso, Texas. Near the barriers are motion sensors and infrared cameras. Stadium lights shine down on the fences, turning night into day.

The barriers do not prevent illegal border crossings. They simply force illegal crossers to move to more remote areas. In the southwest, that means hot, waterless deserts. Border fences also prompt the digging of tunnels. Many of these tunnels extend for long distances, and allow illegal immigrants to easily evade the Border Patrol.

The illegal border crossings have brought environmental damage and higher crime rates to the areas near the U.S.–Mexico line. One witness, Leo Banks, explained:

> Ranchers in hard-hit areas spend the first hours of every day repairing damage done the night before. They find fences knocked down and water spigots left on, draining thousands of precious gallons. . . . One rancher told me about illegals who rustled one of her newborn calves. The intruders beat the twelve-hour-old animal to death with a fence post, then barbecued it on the spot.[2]

Since 1995, about twenty-six hundred people have died of thirst, exposure, and violence while crossing the border between the United States and Mexico.[3] In 2005, the Border Patrol caught 1.2 million illegal border-crossers—about one arrest every thirty seconds.[4] Usually the crossers are apprehended, sent through a processing station, and then driven back across the border. The Border Patrol refers to this procedure as "catch and release."

The southern border presents the United States—particularly California, Arizona, New Mexico, and Texas—with a serious dilemma. Where the border is unfenced, illegal crossings result in crime, environmental damage, and the deaths of people unprepared for the harsh desert conditions. In addition, some believe the southern border provides terrorists intent on violent and criminal acts an easy way to enter the United States.

Some say the solution is to make the barrier fence complete and permanent. In 2005, members of Congress proposed a new barrier that would extend along the entire U.S.–Mexican border. There would be a 100-yard zone on the U.S. side of the border. In this zone, the Border Patrol would have the authority to question and detain anyone found there.

The Secure Fence Act of 2006 passed the House and Senate in September 2006. The law partially funded construction of 700 miles of fence. It increased the number of Border Patrol agents. It added beds to detention facilities to end the "catch and release" method of handling illegal aliens.

President Bush signed the law in October 2006. The president

> The southern border presents the United States with a serious dilemma. Illegal crossings result in crime, environmental damage, and the deaths of people unprepared for the harsh desert conditions.

commented then that, "We have a responsibility to address these challenges. We have a responsibility to enforce our laws. We have a responsibility to secure our borders. We take this responsibility seriously."[5]

The government of Mexico opposes the fence. Its view is that increased border security only makes the trip across the border more dangerous and results in needless deaths. Mexico in general favors more open borders and easier immigration, which ultimately benefits poor Mexican families.

There is strong sentiment against the border fence in the United States as well. Hispanic leaders in the United States, in particular, do not want the barrier. Hector M. Flores, of the League of United Latin American Citizens, said:

> I wonder what U.S. citizens would do if this part of our labor force were actually deterred by the fences, workplace raids, and other anti-immigrant policies that Congress is considering. Does the anti-immigrant crowd actually expect that unemployed Americans will step forward and accept those low-pay, long-hour, back-breaking jobs that offer no benefits, no overtime, and no vacations? . . . Will anyone stop to wonder why the heck we did this to ourselves when all we had to do was to provide for a legal avenue for these workers to come here in the first place?[6]

Illegal immigrants are placed in holding facilities before being returned to Mexico. There is great disagreement over the best way to prevent illegal entry.

Some people opposed to illegal immigration have taken matters into their own hands. An extremist group called the Minutemen set up operations in April 2005. Their volunteers drove to the border in Cochise County, Arizona. They kept in contact with the Border Patrol and reported on persons suspected to be illegal border-crossers. Their rules were not to approach illegals. They stayed at the border for one month.

The Minutemen drew both support and opposition. Some people thought of them as vigilantes—people intent on violence who were taking the law into their own hands. The mayor of Douglas, Arizona, explained:

> I think they are adventure-seekers. There's no danger involved for them. They are the ones packing the arms and looking important. There's no bravery there. There's no patriotism there. These people can't fight back and aren't gonna fight back; they're on their way to work. If the people *were* coming over here armed and they *were* fighting back, then we'd see how many volunteers [they would] get.[7]

A few saw them as heroes, risking their safety to protect the United States from a hostile invasion, and doing the necessary work that the federal government will not or cannot do.

7 A Global Economy

Some commentators on the immigration debate see newcomers as endangering American society. According to this view, immigrants from many countries are not interested in assimilation. Instead, they are creating a hostile, alien community within the United States, threatening the well-being of the native-born. "America has become a nation of broken borders," comments Lou Dobbs, a CNN reporter and author of the book *War on the Middle Class.* "People enter our country seemingly at will, without regard for our laws. They threaten our safety and security, they use our resources, and they take our jobs."[1]

This argument is older than the United States itself. It was once thought that Germans (then Irish, then Chinese, then Italians, then eastern Europeans, then Japanese) would never identify themselves as Americans and never accept the new society and culture that surrounded them. It was also thought that African Americans, the descendants of slaves, would never be able to join the American mainstream.

Now the threat is Mexico, according to political scientist Samuel Huntington:

> If over one million Mexican soldiers crossed the border Americans would treat it as a major threat to their national security and react accordingly. The invasion of over one million Mexican civilians . . . would be a comparable threat. . . . Mexican immigration is a unique, disturbing, and looming challenge to our cultural integrity, our national identity, and potentially to our future as a country.[2]

Author Michael Barone disagrees with this outlook:

> Our largest source of immigrants is Mexico, and it is true that you can see Latinos in Los Angeles root for Mexico in the World Cup and wave Mexican flags in demonstrations against crackdowns on illegal immigration. But the number of Mexican immigrants who want to bring the Mexican system of law and government to the United States is minuscule. The overwhelming majority of Latin— and Asian—immigrants are interested primarily in work.[3]

A Shock to the Immigration System

The terrorist attacks of 9/11 had a drastic effect on immigration. In March 2003, the INS was abolished and the new United States Citizenship and Immigration Services (USCIS) was established. The USCIS, and all other immigration and customs agencies, became part of the Department of Homeland Security (DHS). An alien-registration program returned, similar to those the government carried out during the two world wars. The procedure for getting a visa became more complicated, more expensive, and much slower.

The Visa Condor program required a security clearance for

every adult male applying for a visa from any of twenty-six Muslim countries. The Visa Mantis program required security clearances for anyone applying for a business visa in certain fields. The government kept a list of these fields on a Technology Alert List. To prevent cheating, the government made the list classified (secret). That means businesspeople have no idea whether or not their visas will be rejected for security reasons.

The new rules on visas discourage people from coming to the United States. Many applicants are rejected for very minor problems on their application forms. Others have trouble meeting their deadlines and keeping to schedules. Discouraged visitors take their business, knowledge, and ability elsewhere.

Handling visas is already overwhelming U.S. consulates and the offices of the USCIS. Most of these agencies do not have enough people to handle the workload. To make matters worse, the USCIS must pay for its operations out of fees it charges applicants. Like the United States Postal Service, it gets no money from the federal government—and it

In 2003, the INS was abolished and the United States Citizenship and Immigration Services (USCIS) was established. Along with all other immigration and customs agencies, it became part of the Department of Homeland Security.

operates in a similar manner. Service is rather slow, and hiring badly needed new staff is difficult.

In Beijing, China, the U.S. consulate conducts more than 700 interviews every day for visa applications.[4] This means the officers can only spend a few minutes with each applicant. The situation is similar in other countries where the demand for visas is high.

Consular officers are cautious. They do not want to make any mistake and issue a visa to the wrong person. Journalist Fareed Zakaria explains: "Every visa officer today lives in fear that he will let in the next Mohammed Atta [the 9/11 terrorist]. As a result, he is probably keeping out the next Bill Gates."[5]

The result is the United States loses out on valuable contacts and exchanges with foreign countries. In addition, skilled people move to countries that compete with the United States for trade and technology. In a global economy, that hurts the competitiveness of the United States. The problems are worst in the system for welcoming foreign students.

Keeping Track of Students

The immigration law of 1996 required the government to set up a system to keep track of foreign students. After the September 2001 attacks, the government improved the system. (Several of the hijackers were holding student visas.) The Student Exchange and Visitor Program (SEVP) began in 2003. The system allows the government to track academic guests, including visiting professors, as well as students who apply on their own or who are part of an exchange program.

U.S. schools that host foreign students are required to participate in this program. They keep track of when the students arrive, what courses they take, where they live and work. They also report to the system when a foreign student changes a major, transfers, drops out, or completes a course of study. If the school loses track of the student, the government is alerted.

After the SEVP began, the number of student applications steeply declined, especially from China and India. Academic departments without the resources or personnel to deal with the program had a hard time correcting false information. Some of them lost teaching assistants, research fellows, and visiting lecturers.

Also, students and teachers who do get visas must have authorization to return to the United States if they leave for vacation or to visit family. This makes it very risky for them to come to the United States. If they cannot return, their school

A CBP officer checks a passenger's ID at Washington-Dulles International Airport. New visa rules were put in place after the events of September 11.

year, or their job, comes to an end. Many people simply will not take the risk.

Other countries, such as Canada and the nations of Western Europe, are much more welcoming than the United States. They are now beating the United States in the race for scholars and researchers. Many business leaders in the United States, including Bill Gates, the chairman of Microsoft, see this as a threat to the country's economic future: "America will find it infinitely more difficult to maintain its technological leadership if it shuts out the very people who are most able to help us compete."[6]

Open Borders

The complex and frustrating visa bureaucracy has inspired calls for reform of the system. Many people also want to see more open borders. Advocates point to the early principles of the United States, and the fact that the country welcomed immigrants in the nineteenth century. This made the United States a place of refuge, and a country that was respected and admired throughout the world.

The visa restrictions after 9/11 caused a steep drop in the number of refugees, businesspeople, students, and other foreigners admitted to the United States. As the borders close, the reputation of America as a refuge for the poor and oppressed disappears. Businesses suffer because their customers, employees, and partners have a hard time traveling to the United States.

Instead of more restrictions, advocates of "open borders" want fewer barriers. They believe simplified immigration laws, and easier immigration, would benefit the United States. As an example, they point to the European Union (EU).

The continent of Europe went through two devastating world wars in the twentieth century. The fighting killed millions of people, destroyed many cities, and wrecked productive industries. After World War II (1939–1945), much of Europe lay in ruins. The United States helped with the Marshall Plan. The program helped European industries rebuild and compete.

In 1992, many of the countries of western Europe formed the European Union. The EU now includes twenty-seven different nations. Trade barriers have come down. So have immigration controls. Citizens of the EU can travel without passports. They can pass freely from one EU country to another. They can live and work where they please.

Some in North America believe the EU can serve as a model for the United States and its neighbors. The countries of North America, including Canada, the United States, and Mexico, should allow freer travel across their borders. This would make a "North American Union" the world's most-powerful economic bloc.

A leading supporter of the open borders idea is Vicente Fox, the former president of Mexico. Fox speaks often about the need to open the border of Mexico and the United States. He pushes the United States to allow Mexicans to cross the border freely.

The Global Market

Business leaders in the United States generally favor a less restrictive immigration policy. They support proposals for a "guest worker" program. They also want an amnesty for illegal immigrants. They believe that without a steady influx of immigrant labor, the U.S. economy will continue to lose competitive ground to low-wage countries.

The globalist argument believes that an international free market in goods is emerging. This market eventually will

A poster from the 1950s shows a very different attitude toward immigration than that expressed in the United States today.

overcome national barriers, including immigration restrictions. It will make a border fence unnecessary—and harmful to the economic well-being of the United States. In the globalist view, increased border security just results in needless deaths and ill will between Mexico and the United States.

Supporters of an open border point out that business is going through an important change. With better communication and transportation, companies can now do business around the world. They can manufacture goods where labor is cheap. They can transport those goods to distant markets. Free trade policies in many countries, including the United States, have ended tariffs (taxes) on imported goods.

According to this argument, freer immigration should come along with the free trade. The United States, in this view, should make it easier for people to visit, to work, and to stay. This includes students, engineers, doctors, nurses, investors, and skilled workers. If immigration to the United States remains costly and time-consuming, people will simply go somewhere else. American companies will lose their technological edge. New and better products will come from factories in China, India, and Europe.

Not all foreign countries can serve as a model for immigration, however. In Europe, countries such as France have experienced turmoil between immigrants and native-born French citizens. Many of these immigrants come from Muslim countries in the Middle East and North Africa, where European nations once had colonies. The foreign language, religion, and culture of the immigrants makes it difficult for them to survive in France and other nations with strong cultural identities of their own.

Other countries have had a much easier experience. Canada, for example, has been able to integrate large numbers of immigrants within its borders with little trouble. England has large numbers of immigrants who were acculturated to the English language and institutions through English colonization of their home countries.

The United States, like England, once welcomed immigrants from former colonies, such as the Philippines. American culture is familiar throughout the world, through movies, books, and television shows. Many foreigners learn English in their schools, and American society is relatively open. Assimilation of immigrant families is a three-hundred-year-old tradition in America, and it is one that will continue no matter what new laws are passed.

A New Immigration Law

8

The issue of immigration has the public's close attention. Many people are demanding a change in the laws. They see a crisis brewing in the United States. Some fear outsiders are overwhelming the United States. Others believe the United States must reform its laws to make immigration easier. Somehow, government agencies must better manage the heavy demand from foreigners seeking to enter the United States, either to visit, to work, or to settle as citizens.

The terrorist attacks of September 11 added the elements of fear and suspicion to the debate. The natural distrust of outsiders and foreign cultures grew stronger. Andrew Greeley, writing in the *Chicago Sun-Times*, observed:

> Since the 9/11 attacks, the endemic hatred of immigrants that has always infected this country has become paranoid. Every immigrant, in the minds of many Americans and especially public officials, has become a potential terrorist. Therefore it is open season on them to the bureaucrats in Homeland Security. Every new immigrant scalp they can gather means more points for their career advancement. Every immigrant family they can break up is another victory for American freedom.[1]

The voters want something done, and so lawmakers are making proposals. But the members of Congress still cannot agree on what to do about people entering the country illegally. The 1986 Immigration Reform and Control Act, which allowed illegal immigrants to stay, did not solve the problem. It gave little opportunity for unskilled workers to enter the country. Employers continued to hire undocumented workers, without penalty. As a result, unskilled workers continued to make their way across the border illegally, by the millions, during the 1990s.

Lawmakers have put forth several immigration bills. Every bill contains dozens of new rules and regulations, and every bill is different. Some grant amnesty for illegal immigrants; some do not. Some allow "guest workers" to become legal residents; some do not. The bills differ on border security, penalties for illegal hiring, and methods of enforcement. Eventually, a new immigration law will pass. Its final effect on immigration, however, is very hard to predict.

Amnesty?

In 2004, President Bush proposed a new program for illegal immigrants. According to the proposal, they could remain in the United States and take part in a guest-worker program. They could pay a fee and prove that they are employed. They could stay for a period of three years. After the end of this period, they could apply for an extension for another three years; only one extension would be allowed. Guest workers, under the Bush proposal, could also apply to become legal permanent residents.

The proposal was greeted with harsh criticism from Bush's own Republican Party. Two dozen Republican congressmen sent the president a letter, which stated in part:

> Our offices have been inundated with calls from dismayed constituents expressing vehement opposition to the Administration's proposal. . . . We cannot continue to allow our immigration laws to be violated and ignored. . . . Illegal aliens are by definition criminals.[2]

Members of Congress answered the president's proposal with ideas of their own. In December 2005, the House of Representatives passed the Border Protection, Anti-Terrorism, and Illegal Immigration Control Act. The law ordered the building of 700 miles of border fence. It would have required the federal government to detain undocumented workers, and ended "catch and release." It would have ended the green-card lottery, and it would have forced employers to electronically verify the legal status of all those applying for work.

This law inspired huge protests in more than 100 cities across the country. Radio personalities, Internet blogs, and newspaper ads urged people to get out to march. Protestors walked in crowds of thousands, holding signs and chanting slogans. Some clashes between protestors and onlookers took place, mostly over the display of Mexican flags.

The new law did not pass the Senate, which then debated a new compromise, the Comprehensive Immigration Reform Act of 2007. This law would have set up a new Z visa for illegal aliens living in the United States on January 1, 2007. The Z visa gave the holder the right to stay in the country, obtain a green card, and eventually win citizenship. A new Y visa was for temporary guest workers, who could stay for two years. The law would have improved border security with more Border Patrol agents, high-tech gear along the southern border, and 300 miles of additional barriers. In the end, President Bush supported the bill.

Another protest began. People opposing amnesty flooded their senators' offices with phone calls and e-mails. The response jammed phone lines and crashed e-mail servers in the U.S. Capitol building. In June 2007, the bill died in the Senate without coming to a vote.

Identifying Workers and Citizens

The debate over a new immigration system died down. There seemed to be no compromise possible between those who wanted to reform the law, and those who simply wanted to enforce a stronger border. Tom Tancredo, a legislator from Colorado, ran for president on the strength of his opposition to the proposed amnesty and illegal immigrants. Tancredo commented:

> I can think of few things that could be more dangerous for homeland security than granting amnesty to 8 to 12 million illegal aliens. Perhaps the administration ought to dedicate more energy to enforcing our existing immigration laws and less on finding ways to allow millions to skirt them.[3]

In the meantime, illegal immigrants continue to arrive. Their services are in demand, and they want to earn more money than is possible at home. They have no trouble finding work. Their services as manual laborers, construction workers, and in restaurants, hotels, and private households are needed. One undocumented worker from Mexico named Maria told author Deepa Fernandes:

> If they were to send us all back to our countries, *this* country would collapse. Who would cook and clean for them? Who would provide them with cheap food, and who would break their backs under the

hot sun in the farms and fields around the country? They need us, because no one else will do this awful and dirty work for so little money.[4]

Employers who break the law by hiring illegal immigrants benefit most from the current system. They can pay low wages, without insurance or other benefits. If they pay cash, they do not pay Social Security taxes. They can ask illegals to work long hours and in unsafe conditions. In the meantime, companies that follow the rules—and pay their workers normal wages and benefits—must pay more for labor. Their products become more expensive and they find it harder to compete.

Many lawmakers point to employers of illegal aliens as the guilty parties in immigration issues. Most proposed immigra-

A CBP agent inspects documents for authenticity. New technological advances have made identification more reliable.

tion laws set higher fines and penalties for employers breaking the law. Under most versions of new immigration laws, employers must take part in a system of electronic verification. They will have to use a central government database to make sure their employees are legal workers.

An important part of any new immigration system will be identification cards and biometric information, such as finger-prints on a readable card. This will allow the government to find illegal aliens, those wanted for visa violations (such as over-stays), and those who have made it onto watch lists of suspected criminals and terrorists.

Some have proposed placing this information onto new Social Security cards. The cards would bear a person's name, date of birth, place of residence, Social Security number, and a photograph. They would also have biometric information, such as fingerprints. Personal information would be contained in a small computer chip. The holder of such a card would not be able to alter or erase the data in the chip.

In 2004, President Bush proposed a new program for illegal immigrants. According to the proposal, they could remain in the United States and take part in a guest-worker program.

In 2005 Congress began debating the REAL ID program. This program would set down guidelines for identification cards and driver's licenses in all fifty states. Before issuing the card, the states must ask for a Social Security number or a document proving the holder's citizenship or status as a legal resident.

Many countries have national ID cards that citizens are supposed to carry at all times. By law, they must show their IDs to any government official who demands to see them. Many nations also expect visitors to carry passports with them, and be ready to show them. A passport is often necessary to exchange money, to get a hotel room, to buy a plane ticket, or rent a car.

No identification is required in the United States. Citizens and tourists can walk about freely without IDs. The law states that permanent residents must carry green cards, but police rarely ask to see a green card. And a national ID card is not a popular idea in the United States. Many people do not want their movements followed or controlled in any way. They do not want personal information available to the authorities.

In his book *The West's Last Chance*, Tony Blankley argues that the time has come for the national biometric ID card. Such a card, in his opinion, would provide the nation with the means to identify foreign terrorists:

> In the age of terror that we have been drawn into, we can no longer afford the luxury of not requiring national identification cards. Without biometric cards for every person living or traveling in the country, even secured borders will be insufficient. This is a war in which information is king, and the ability to positively identify people is a necessary component of our defense.[5]

Sanctions and Sanctuary

Another issue lawmakers must solve is the problem of jurisdiction. For more than a century, immigration has been a federal matter. The national government arrests illegal immigrants and takes care of border control. Local police and state governments have nothing to do with immigration enforcement. Police departments, in general, see immigration enforcement as interfering with their normal work. Craig Ferrell, a member of the Houston Police Department, explained:

> Police need immigrants to feel comfortable talking to authorities and not fear deportation. . . . There are lots of people with a questionable immigration status. . . . They are witnesses to crimes. It's important to have assistance from law-abiding people to solve crimes and keep the city safe.[6]

Some cities are protesting federal immigration policy by providing "sanctuary." They prohibit the arrest of residents

A demonstrator expresses pro-immigrant sentiments. Some people and cities are resisting federal immigration policies by offering sanctuary to undocumented immigrants.

on immigration matters. They do not allow their police to ask immigration questions of people who are arrested or stopped for any reason. Sanctuary cities include San Francisco, St. Paul, and New York City. The states of Alaska and Oregon have passed laws that bar state workers from enforcing federal immigration laws.

The sanctuary issue highlights the tension between local and federal authorities over immigration. In the future, many more issues will arise. Do states have the authority to pass immigration laws of their own? Can the local police arrest and detain immigration violators? Can cities become sanctuaries for undocumented workers? Can the states set immigration quotas? Can they issue visas? If federal law does not answer the questions, they must be decided in court.

In some proposed new law, state and local authorities will be able to make their own decisions. In others, these same authorities will lose federal funding if they do not enforce federal law.

Elections and Change

Politics and the lawmaking process make it very difficult for immigration proposals to become law. According to the U.S. Constitution, laws are first passed in the House of Representatives. Competing bills are passed in the Senate. The bills go through a process of amendment (change). Committees reconcile the differences between the House and Senate bills.

When the bill finally passes both houses of Congress, it goes to the President for signature. It then becomes federal law. If the president vetoes (rejects) the law, it goes back to Congress. The members of Congress can override the veto with a two-thirds majority, make more changes in the law and pass a different version, or drop the matter.

In the meantime, many different ideas come forth. Lawmakers are under pressure from the voters to pass a law. They want to show that their own party, and not the opposition, has better ideas and is more effective. This means seemingly endless debate and compromise. Original ideas change and are sometimes dropped.

After the election of 2006, pressure mounted for a new immigration law. Candidates looking to the elections of 2008 put forth their ideas and opinions. Immigration again became a political hot potato.

The issue inspires passion and anger. Immigration lies at the heart of U.S. history and the identity of the country. That is because American society is constantly changing, thanks to the arrival of foreigners with their new ideas and new cultures. The immigration decisions now being made will largely shape the future of the United States.

Chronology

1798—By the Alien Enemies Act, the U.S. Congress gives the president the authority to deport enemy aliens during wartime.

1840s—A wave of Irish immigration begins in the eastern United States.

1868—The Fourteenth Amendment to the U.S. Constitution grants citizenship to anyone born in the United States.

1882—The Chinese Exclusion Act bars all immigrants from China, with the exception of merchants.

1890s—A second wave of immigration from southern and eastern Europe begins. Immigrants begin passing through Ellis Island, a station for processing newcomers in New York harbor.

1914—World War I begins in Europe, and immigration from that continent nearly stops.

1917—Congress passes a literacy test for immigrants, and overrides President Wilson's veto of the new law.

1921—The Johnson Act is passed, setting quotas for immigrants depending on their country of origin.

1924—The Johnson-Reed Act sets stricter national-origin quotas for immigrants.

1929—A stock market crash touches off the Great Depression. With unemployment high, immigration to the United States slows.

1940—The Smith Act requires all aliens over age fourteen to register with the Immigration and Naturalization Service (INS).

1952—The McCarran-Walter Act allows any foreign national to apply for citizenship. The Texas Proviso makes it lawful to hire illegal immigrants to work in the United States.

1953—The Refugee Relief Act sets a separate immigration quota for political refugees from Communist nations.

1965—The Hart-Celler Act ends national-origin quotas. New quotas are created for immigrants from the eastern and western hemispheres.

1986—The Immigration Reform and Control Act grants amnesty to illegal aliens living in the United States since 1982 or earlier.

1994—Operation Gatekeeper reinforces border security in California and begins the construction of a barrier to keep out illegal immigrants.

1996—The H-1B visa is introduced to allow skilled workers to stay in the United States for three years.

2001—The USA PATRIOT Act is passed, setting stricter guidelines for immigration and requiring background checks on new immigrants.

2006—The Secure Fence Act is passed by Congress, authorizing construction of a 700-mile barrier on the U.S.-Mexico border.

Chapter Notes

Chapter 1. A Land of Newcomers

1. Howard B. Furer, *The Germans in America, 1607–1970* (Dobbs Ferry, N.Y.: Oceana Publications, 1973), p. 91.

2. Roger Daniels, *Coming to America: A History of Immigration and Ethnicity in American Life* (New York: Harper Perennial, 2002), p. 130.

3. Thomas Sowell, *Ethnic America: A History* (New York: Basic Books, 1981), p. 34.

4. "*Chae Chan Ping* v. *United States*," © 1995, <http://tourolaw.edu/Patch/Chae/> (November 6, 2007).

5. Andrew Gyory, *Closing the Gate: Race, Politics, and the Chinese Exclusion Act* (Chapel Hill, N.C.: University of North Carolina Press, 1998), p. 3.

6. Ellis Island National Memorial, National Park Service, October 16, 2007, <http://www.nps.gov/elis/> (November 6, 2007).

7. David M. Brownstone, Irene M. Franck, and Douglass Brownstone, *Island of Hope, Island of Tears: The Story of Those Who Entered the New World through Ellis Island—In Their Own Words* (New York: MetroBooks, 2000), p. 172.

Chapter 2. Twentieth-Century Immigration

1. "The Zimmerman Telegram," n.d., <http://www.geocities.com/Colosseum/Park/8386/zman.htm> (September 29, 2007).

2. Leonard Gelber, *Dictionary of American History* (Lanham, Md.: Rowman and Littlefield, 1978), p. 523.

3. David Mauk and John Oakland, *American Civilization: An Introduction* (New York: Routledge, 2005), p. 60.

4. Michele Wucker, *Lockout: Why America Keeps Getting Immigration Wrong When Our Prosperity Depends on Getting it Right* (New York: Public Affairs, 2006), p. 82.

5. "Displaced Persons," USHMM.org, October 25, 2007, <http://

www.ushmm.org/wlc/article.php?lang=en&ModuleId=10005462>
(November 6, 2007).

6. "1940s: Displaced Persons Act of 1948," *Documents of American History II*, April 29, 2002, <http://tucnak.fsv.cuni.cz/~calda/Documents/1940s/Displaced%20Persons%20Act%20of%201948.html> (February 28, 2008).

7. "Three Decades of Mass Immigration: The Legacy of the 1965 Immigration Act," *Center for Immigration Studies*, n.d., <http://www.cis.org/articles/1995/back395.html> (September 29, 2007).

8. Patrick J. Buchanan, *State of Emergency: The Third World Invasion and Conquest of America* (New York: Thomas Dunne Books, 2006), p. 239.

Chapter 3. Illegal Immigration

1. Donald L. Bartlett and James P. Steele, "Who Left the Door Open?" *Time*, September 20, 2004, p. 54.

2. Deepa Fernandes, *Targeted: Homeland Security and the Business of Immigration* (New York: Seven Stories Press, 2007), p. 44.

3. Herman Badillo, *One Nation, One Standard: An Ex-Liberal on How Hispanics Can Succeed Just Like Other Immigrant Groups* (New York: Sentinel, 2006), pp. 212–213.

Chapter 4. Immigration and the U.S. Economy

1. "INS Questions Meatpacking Workers as Part of Operation Vanguard," *National Immigration Law Center*, n.d., <http://www.nilc.org/immsemplymnt/wkplce_enfrcmnt/wkplcenfrc008.htm> (September 29, 2007).

2. Michael Barone, *The New Americans: How the Melting Pot Can Work Again* (Washington, D.C.: Regnery Publishing, 2001), p. 150.

3. "What Kind of Work Do Immigrants Do?" *Migration Policy Institute*, January 2004, <http://migrationpolicy.org/pubs/Foreign%20Born%20Occup%20and%20Industry%20in%20the%20US.pdf> (September 29, 2007).

4. Vernon M. Briggs, Jr., and Stephen Moore, *Still an Open Door?*

U.S. Immigration Policy and the American Economy (Washington, D.C.: The American University Press, 1994), p. 77.

5. Daphne Spain, "The Debate in the United States Over Immigration," n.d., <http://usinfo.state.gov/journals/itsv/0699/ijse/spain.htm> (September 29, 2007).

Chapter 5. Visas and Citizenship

1. "Current Cap Count for Non-Immigrant Worker Visas for Fiscal Year 2008," *United States Citizenship and Immigration Service*, n.d., <http://www.uscis.gov/portal/site/uscis/menuitem.5af9bb95919f35 e66f614176543f6d1a/?vgnextoid=138b6138f898d010VgnVCM10 000048f3d6a1RCRD&vgnextchannel=91919c7755cb9010VgnVC M10000045f3d6a1RCRD> (September 29, 2007).

2. "Oath of Allegiance for Naturalized Citizens," United States Citizenship and Immigration Service, n.d., <http://www.uscis.gov/portal/site/uscis/menuitem.5af9bb95919f35e66f614176543f6d1a/? vgnextoid=931696981298d010VgnVCM10000048f3d6a1RCRD &vgnextchannel=d6f4194d3e88d010VgnVCM10000048f3d6a1R CRD> (September 29, 2007).

3. Samuel P. Huntington, *Who Are We? The Challenges to America's National Identity* (New York: Simon & Schuster, 2004), p. 206.

4. "Visa Waiver Program," *U.S. Department of State*, October 2007, <http://travel.state.gov/visa/temp/without/without_1990.html> (September 29, 2007).

Chapter 6. A Threat to the United States?

1. Vince Beiser, "Separated by Law: How the Immigration Service is Breaking Up Families," *The Progressive*, vol. 71, no. 9, September 2007, p. 21.

2. J. D. Hayworth, *Whatever it Takes: Illegal Immigration, Border Security, and the War on Terror* (Washington, D.C.: Regnery Publishing, 2006), p. 12.

3. Deepa Fernandes, *Targeted: Homeland Security and the Business of Immigration* (New York: Seven Stories Press, 2007), p. 50.

4. Dannielle Blumenthal, "At 3rd Anniversary, CBP Builds on

Security Successes," *U.S. Customs and Border Protection*, n.d., <http://www.cbp.gov/xp/CustomsToday/2006/March/3rd_anniversary.xml> (September 29, 2007).

5. "President Bush Signs Secure Fence Act," *The White House*, n.d., <http://www.whitehouse.gov/news/releases/2006/10/20061026.html> (September 29, 2007).

6. Hector M. Flores, "The Wall of Shame," *League of United Latin American Citizens*, January 3, 2006 <http://www.lulac.org/advocacy/press/2006/wallofshame.html> (November 6, 2007).

7. Bob Moser, "Civilian Patrols Endanger Illegal Immigrants," in Margaret Haerens, ed., *Illegal Immigration* (Farmington Hills, Mich.: Greenhaven Press, 2006), p. 145.

Chapter 7. A Global Economy

1. Lou Dobbs, *War on the Middle Class* (New York: Penguin Books, 2006), p. 134.

2. Samuel Huntington, "Reconsidering Immigration: Is Mexico a Special Case?" *Center for Immigration Studies*, November 2000, <http://www.cis.org/articles/2000/back1100.html> (September 29, 2007).

3. Michael Barone, *The New Americans: How the Melting Pot Can Work Again* (Washington, D.C.: Regnery Publishing, 2001), p. x.

4. James S. Langer, "Impact of Post 9-11 Visa Policies on Science and Technology," *The National Academies*, n.d., <http://www7.nationalacademies.org/visas/LangerSTCaucus.pdf> (September 29, 2007).

5. Michele Wucker, *Lockout: Why America Keeps Getting Immigration Wrong When Our Prosperity Depends on Getting it Right* (New York: Public Affairs, 2006), p. 155.

6. Alan Greenspan, *The Age of Turbulence* (New York: The Penguin Press, 2007), p. 407.

Chapter 8. A New Immigration Law

1. Andrew Greeley, *Chicago Sun-Times*, June 10, 2005, quoted in

Margaret Haerens, ed., *Illegal Immigration* (Farmington Hills, Mich.: Greenhaven Press, 2006), p. 93.

2. Gordon Hanson, *Why Does Immigration Divide America?: Public Finance and Political Opposition to Open Borders* (Washington, D.C.: Institute for International Economics, 2005), p. 2.

3. Quoted in Haerens, p. 165.

4. Deepa Fernandes, *Targeted: Homeland Security and the Business of Immigration* (New York: Seven Stories Press, 2007) p. 45.

5. Tony Blankley, *The West's Last Chance: Will We Win the Clash of Civilizations?* (Washington, D.C.: Regnery Publishing, 2005), p. 174.

6. Dick Morris & Eileen McGann, *Outrage* (New York: HarperCollins, 2007), p. 33.

Glossary

amnesty—A law that would allow illegal immigrants to remain in the United States.

assimilate—To become absorbed into a culture, adopting its language and customs.

bilingualism—A program of teaching in two languages.

biometrics—Physical information unique to each individual, such as fingerprints and retinal scans, which can be used to identify and track people.

bracero—Guest-worker programs begun during World War II that brought Mexicans temporarily into the southwestern United States to work. The bracero program ended in 1964.

Cable Act—A 1922 federal law that allowed women who married foreigners to remain U.S. citizens, provided they did not leave the country.

chain migration—The phenomenon of immigrants establishing themselves in the United States and then hosting members of their family as new immigrants in the following years.

Chinese Exclusion Act (1882)—A federal law that barred Chinese immigrants, except merchants.

Dillingham Commission—A congressional committee that studied the issue of immigration in the early twentieth century, and which recommended national-origins quotas.

Displaced Persons Act (1948)—A law that allowed political refugees to enter the United States under a separate quota system.

Emergency Quota Act—(also known as the Johnson Act; 1921)—An immigration law that established quotas for new arrivals according to their country of origin. The number of immigrants from each nation depended on the percentage of foreign-born from that nation in the United States in 1910.

Gentlemen's Agreement (1907)—A treaty with Japan that barred Japanese immigrants from the United States.

guest worker—An immigrant who is allowed to remain in the United States for the purpose of working.

Hart-Celler Act (1965)—An immigration law that ended the system of national-origins quotas.

head tax—A fee charged to shipping companies for each immigrant brought to the United States.

I-9—A document all employers must provide for new employees, which shows they are authorized to work in the United States.

I-94—A document filled out by foreign visitors when they enter the United States from abroad.

Immigration and Naturalization Service (INS)—The former immigration agency of the United States. It was abolished in 2003, and its functions were given to three new agencies: the United States Citizenship and Immigration Services (USCIS), Immigration and Customs Enforcement (ICE), and Customs and Border Protection (CBP).

indenture system—A system originating in colonial times, in which immigrants agreed to service for a period of years as payment for their passage to North America.

McCarran-Walter Act (1952)—An immigration law that set an upper limit of 270,000 immigrants per year, in addition to family members and refugees.

National Origins Quota Act (also known as the Johnson-Reed Act; 1924)—An immigration law that changed the national-origins quota to match the percentage of foreign-born in 1890.

Refugee Act (1980)—A federal law that allowed refugees to immigrate to the United States on a regular basis, subject to an annual quota.

Refugee Relief Act (1953)—A law allowing refugees from Communist regimes in Europe to immigrate to the United States.

Simpson-Mazzoli Act (1986)—Also known as the Immigration Reform and Control Act, this law granted a blanket amnesty to undocumented workers who had lived in the U.S. continuously since before January 1, 1982. The law also made it illegal to knowingly hire illegal immigrants.

Smith Act (1940)—A law passed after the start of World War II in Europe that set up a registration program for all noncitizens.

sojourners—Immigrants who arrive temporarily, solely for the purpose of work, and then return to their home country.

visa—Formal permission for a person to enter a foreign country, granted by that country's government. Visas are inspected and approved by government officials at the point of entry.

Further Reading

Books

Allport, Alan. *Immigration Policy*. Philadelphia: Chelsea House, 2005.

Gibney, Matthew J. and Randall Hansen, eds. *Immigration and Asylum: From 1900 to the Present*. Santa Barbara, Calif.: ABC-CLIO, 2005.

Hunter, Miranda. *Latino Americans and Immigration Laws: Crossing the Border*. Philadelphia: Mason Crest Publishers, 2006.

Miller, Debra A. *Illegal Immigration*. San Diego: ReferencePoint Press, 2007.

Powell, John. *Encyclopedia of North American Immigration*. New York: Facts on File, 2005.

Wepman, Dennis. *Immigration: From the Founding of Virginia to the Closing of Ellis Island*. New York: Facts on File, 2002.

Internet Addresses

NumbersUSA
   <http://www.numbersusa.com>

United States Immigration Support
   <http://www.usimmigrationsupport.org>

U.S. Customs and Border Protection
   <http://www.cbp.gov/xp/cgov/home.xml>

Index